----- *WHAT OT*

"*Relationships Matter! Giving for Impact joins the hands of the donor with the hands of the nonprofit to make a meaningful impact. Giving for Impact has helped me find not only my core passions and calling to invest my life in, but how to find and maintain the type of relationships with nonprofits that know that there is more to me than my finances.*"

— MARK B. WEAVER
President, Transformational Generosity

"*Jamie's book challenges the donor and the nonprofit organization to truly examine themselves and each other in pursuit of building authentic, holistic relationships. This simple, yet strategic guide will help donors become more impactful givers and organizations to become more effective in delivering their mission.*"

— CLAYTON BOYLES
Executive Director, Dubois County Community Foundation

GIVING
FOR
IMPACT

$$\text{(person)} + NPO + \text{(people)} = Impact$$

JAMIE LEVY

ISBN-13: 978-1-7336375-4-1 (JDLevy & Associates)

JDLevy & Associates, Inc.
PMB 102
3557 N. Newton Street
Jasper, IN 47546

jdlevyassociates.com

In my years studying, teaching and consulting on the topic on philanthropy, I am amazed at how many people, while truly desiring it, have not found a place of true impact through their giving. Creating impact, or Giving for Impact, is central to my life and work, and is very personal to me. Helping people discover themselves and their unique expressions of creating value in the world around them. Creating impact through giving does not simply happen. It requires a journey of discovery. As you journey through this book, remember that creating impact is also about you, not just those you seek to help. Changed lives for both the giver and receiver. Philanthropy, at its core, is a discovery of the passion for how we can best love those around us. The world will be a better place because of your impact.

Thank you,

Jamie D. Levy
Jeremiah 33:3

CONTENTS

YOU WANT TO MAKE A DIFFERENCE. NOW WHAT?

Know yourself
+
Know the
organization
+
Know what
partnership
looks like
=
Meaningful
Impact

You Want To Make A Difference. Now What?

The world is broken and you want to make a difference.

That is why you are opening a book about "giving for impact" isn't it? You want to make an impact in the world. You want to spend your one and only life shining light in the darkness.

It may be impact for a cause, for a community, or for a culture.

Whether you are a donor, potential donor, board member, or nonprofit staff member, you have a heart to help make things better in some way. You want to create change.

Unfortunately, that passion can easily express itself through merely writing checks to a variety of organizations for which you feel may not have a lasting impact. You give when asked, but may not feel like you are making the difference for which you are uniquely wired.

It can, therefore, be unfulfilling. Sure, it feels good to give, but how do you know your gifts are truly making a difference? Is there a way to be more meaningfully involved in the cause? Is it truly fulfilling your passions and vision? Does it line up with your personal values?

There must be something more to this giving thing, right?

I have good news, there is.

I believe philanthropy is the greatest way to create change in our world.

Philanthropy not only provides change for a cause, but also has the power to change you as you explore what it means to be meaningfully involved in creating that change.

Donors share they often feel they are just writing checks. They are unsure if they are making a difference, question if they are adding value to their community, or wonder if they are even being a wise steward of their resources.

One of the biggest reasons donors stop giving to charitable nonprofits is they simply feel no one values having a relationship with them. Donors also can feel limited with their current involvement with nonprofts. These realities can be frustrating, but there are solutions to the frustrations.

Andy, a donor who had given significantly to an organization for several years, was frustrated. He had been impacted by the organization as a youth, and recongized the organization's positive and lasting impact on his siblings and friends. As an adult, he volunteered with the organization. He gave financially. He advocated for their value in the community. He referred people to them for their services. He considered himself highly committed to the organization's success and would do most anything to help them achieve their goals.

Yet, each year when he would receive their annual fall appeal letter, it would be addressed, "Dear Friend." It was a small thing, but this general reference rather than a personal greeting made him feel as if he was just a number. He felt the organization did not really see him as a valued partner. He knew them, but he was not sure they actually knew him. As a caring and committed donor, this caused him frustration.

This book is an opportunity for us to explore together what making an impact can look like. We will address ways you can partner with nonprofit organizations to create change, and discover your personal vision and fulfillment, as you step into the unique role you are wired to play.

+ NPO + = Impact

The principles in this book are worth pursuing. How you can create significant change is worth learning. Your vision for something better in the world is worth getting excited about.

Equation For Impact

Philanthropy is about impact. It is about loving people in a way that improves their lives. I believe the key to creating true and lasting impact in philanthropy boils down to one simple equation:

**KNOW YOURSELF
+ KNOW THE ORGANIZATION
+ KNOW WHAT PARTNERSHIP LOOKS LIKE
= MEANINGFUL IMPACT**

This "equation for impact" is what we will spend the rest of this book investigating. As you learn how to truly understand what is important to you in giving, the unique role of nonprofit organizations and how to define what a healthy giving partnership looks like, then you will discover how to create the greatest change for the cause(s) you have a heart call to impact.

It's About Relationships

Philanthropy fascinates me, because it shows us, when we understand it, how we can truly express our love of people. It has the power to change entire cultures and provide creative solutions for societal issues. Both through academics and experience, my professional life has been dedicated to philanthropy.

In addition to teaching on this topic, I also lead a consultancy which works in the nonprofit sector in two main ways:

1. *Helping nonprofits create long-term sustainability in their organization.*
2. *Helping donors understand how to more effectively create change around the issue(s) and cause(s) they invest in.*

Working on both sides of the giving "equation" allows me a unique vantage point to see the barriers and the opportunities of both nonprofit organizations and donors (large and small). Improved understanding on both sides will increase, and even multiply, impact to cause(s) where values align.

A healthy partnership can lead to real change in our communities and the world. To accomplish this, it all boils down to relationships. When donors and nonprofits can develop healthy, win-win relationships around the cause they love, giving is more meaningful, impact is greater and organizations are stronger. Everyone wins.

A donor told me this story:

"For years, my husband and I were inundated with requests for donations through mailers and individuals asking for donations for capital campaigns, blitzes, and events. We would write a token check because we heard "they do good work" and then we would move on to the next request. There was rarely much satisfaction in what we were doing. We gave to organizations that we were not that interested in but felt we had to give something because we were asked.

At one point, within about a year's time, we had two very unsettling experiences with two separate well-established non-profits where our time and money was not wisely used. We felt taken advantage of. It was at that point we vowed never to let ourselves get into that situation again.

We decided to be more diligent in identifying our own passions and learning more about the non-profits who served those passions. That meant we had to ask the non-profits lots of questions regarding how they operated.

We now meet with the Executive Director and often the Board Chair to ask many questions about the non-profit before we ever consider making our larger donations.

Once the nonprofits are identified and we have taken the time to get to know them and for them to know us, we then determine what aspects of the organization we want to support. Through these conversations, we sometimes see areas within the organization that could be improved upon. Maybe it is additional training of staff, or better-equipped offices, or enhancement of a certain aspect of their mission that would allow them to better serve the population they are working with.

We took the time to understand who we are as donors. Where do our passions lay? Who are the organizations addressing those passions? How can we go about being in partnership with the nonprofit to allow them to have the greatest impact?

We are no longer just check writers. We feel we are making a measurable difference in our community by supporting the experts in the field. We are much more strategic, which brings so much more satisfaction as donors than we had in the past."

A healthy partnership between a donor and a nonprofit organization they support is not about money. It is not about time. It is about relationships -- holistic relationships.

When you are in a healthy relationship with an organization, you will grow personally as you discover the most meaningful ways to engage around the cause you feel called to support. It is not simply the nonprofit asking you for more money. It is investing your heart, your abilities, and your resources into the cause.

When the connection is right, you are afforded the opportunity to create lasting impact filled with purpose that allows you to point to specific and meaningful results. You are simultaneously engaging your heart, beliefs and values. You are taking part in something larger than yourself.

The nonprofit is a vehicle which connects you and other like-minded people to a cause. When you "unearth" and discover your best fit in the cause, you will make the most impact. When you are fully investing yourself in the cause, through thinking about it and engaging your heart in it, then you are not simply giving funds to let someone else do the work. You are a part of the work, a partner in the process. Ideally, you are a long-term partner working with the organization to make a long-term impact.

🧍 + NPO + 👫 = *Impact*

This is a critically different perspective than simply writing checks from a distance. Instead, you are in a relationship, together working and interacting around the cause with the nonprofit.

This book is designed to help you find that fit. To help you create impact around the cause(s) which align with your passion and values.

Because, let's be honest, there are plenty of bad fits. There are nonprofit organizations who do not share your values nor operate in a way that connects with you. This does not mean the organization is doing something wrong. It just means it is not the right fit for you personally.

In this book, you will be equipped with tools to:
- *Recognize a good nonprofit fit when you find one, and tools for when you do not.*
- *Identify red flags in nonprofits who might not be operating in a relational or professional manner.*
- *Create a map of your personal giving philosophy which can lead you to meaningful and impactful relationships to make a long-term difference.*

When you and others are working together within your strengths, finding your fit in philanthropy, true change can happen.

Impact

To begin, we will explore the three main themes from the equation for impact:

1. *Know yourself*
2. *Know the organization*
3. *Know how to build healthy partnerships/relationships with the nonprofit*

But before we move further, let's make sure we understand what "philanthropy" means.

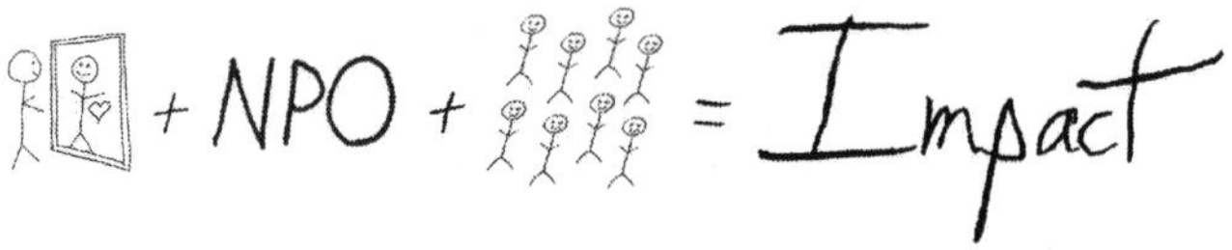

**KNOW YOURSELF
+ KNOW THE ORGANIZATION
+ KNOW WHAT PARTNERSHIP LOOKS LIKE
= MEANINGFUL IMPACT**

What Is Philanthropy?

Philanthropy literally means "love of man or humanity."

It comes from the Greek root words "philos" and "philein" meaning, "loving" and "to love." "Anthro" comes from the Greek word for "humanity" or "man." Love of humankind.

Philanthropy is not a transactional pursuit of money. Philanthropy is an outlet for people to express their love. It is a place where society can invest in their values.

This can range from education to health to business innovation, to art, faith, athletics, politics, poverty, agriculture and far beyond.

Let's say you love cats.

You have cats, you read about cats, you tell other people about cats. You believe the world would be a better place if there were more cats, healthier cats, and more education about cats.

Philanthropy is the way through which you could express your love for cats.

You can find an organization dedicated to cats. Let's call it the Cat Coalition. You can meet other like-minded cat lovers. You can hold educational meetings about cats. You can rescue stray cats and find them homes. You can donate your finances to support the Cat Coalition. You can serve on committees to strategize about improving cat health in your community. You can find meaning and fulfillment through your involvement with these cat activities. The Cat Coalition helps connect you to that meaning, passion and fulfillment.

It's a win-win relationship.

The Cat Coalition, and therefore the cat cause, wins by having another advocate, volunteer, and donor on the team. You win by having an outlet to express your love for cats in a deeper way than you could on your own.

You each receive value from the relationship.

This is philanthropy.

Unfortunately, our vision of philanthropy has become lessened by improper efforts of some nonprofits. Rather than helping people understand the true purpose of the organization's cause and inviting individuals to invest themselves in a greater purpose, we have lessened it by using guilt, coercion, or influence to raise funds. Often the focus is on begging and seeing people as a commodity to be won, by trying to sell them on a quick gift to fix a certain current issue, as opposed to engaging them in a holistic relationship. In this cheapened view held by some in the nonprofit sector, relationships are viewed as disposable.

Instead, true philanthropy builds life-giving relationships on both sides.

While the cat illustration is a simple analogy, the impact of philanthropy cannot be overstated. Throughout history we see this love of people expressed in parents adopting an orphan, in the founding of universities, in a musician creating beautiful music, the work to abolish slavery, someone mowing their neighbor's lawn, or the building of hospitals. Love for people is seen in big and small ways in all areas of life.

Philanthropy is much larger than writing a check. It is living life with intentionally, with meaning, discovering how to create the greatest change for the cause(s) you have a genuine heart call to impact.

The Charitable Sector

While it is easy to think of philanthropy being reserved for the wealthy, the truth is:

- *The large majority of the U.S. population gives and volunteers their time with charitable causes.*[1]
- *The more families earn, the larger the gifts, but the smaller percentage of income they give. For the families families who earn less, they give higher percentages of their incomes to charity.*[2]

Philanthropy is a major part of our economy. It expresses itself in what we call the charitable (nonprofit) sector. This means nonprofit organizations work in a different area in our economy than business or government. Nonprofits provide services that promote the public good. They step into a gap in society that government cannot meet and where business typically cannot make a profit and/or do with the same quality while maintaining trust from society.

Nonprofits Operate At A Financial Loss

Nonprofits, by definition, typically operate at a financial loss in their mission-favored activities. Though nonprofits do and should generate a profit, that profit must go back into its programs. This does not mean the organization manages funds poorly or is in debt. It means that nonprofits are not structured to make a financial gain by the services they offer. Therefore, they require other revenue streams, such as donors, government, earned income, endowments, fee for service, etc. for funding their services.

For example, the Cat Coalition could not fund their stray cat rescue efforts by charging people to rescue cats. The cats typically cannot afford it either :). There is not a way to make money rescuing cats, yet the organization believes there is a need and benefit to society for these cats to be rescued. Therefore, people who have a passion for these stray cats donate their time and finances to rescue them.

Because business cannot find a way to monetize this effort and cat rescuing does not fall under the jurisdiction of government, the Cat Coalition works in the charitable sector to provide value to their community.

Nonprofits Provide Shared Values

Nonprofits often have a caricature of being a beggar asking for funds through a one-sided relationship. Donors take the role of giver and nonprofits take the role of receiver, always taking from these donors.

However, true philanthropy provides value to both sides of the donor and nonprofit relationship. It's a win-win value exchange. The nonprofit receives additional resources to support the cause as new partners join their work. Donors receive meaning and fulfillment as they discover how to express their love of people in ways they could not do without the organization.

For-profit businesses operate on exchanging value. You trade four dollars to the coffee shop for a Cafe' Americano. In the same way, nonprofits operate on an exchange of value. Nonprofits are designed to work as a matchmaker, connecting the donor in a win-win relationship to a shared cause. A donor makes a gift in exchange for the opportunity to impact society. This exchange is a new concept for many and can be the key in understanding true philanthropy.

Where Your Deep Gladness Meets The World's Deep Hunger

Frederick Buechner, a writer and theologian, said "The place God calls you to is the place where your deep gladness and the world's deep hunger meet."

A nonprofit helps connect you to your calling. Your "deep gladness" meets the world's "deep hunger."

I love this description because it implies the fact the donor and organization are in a mutual relationship. Like we said earlier, both win. The donor receives the value of being able to express their love of people through a cause. The organization receives the value of the donor's gifts, resources and passions to further their common mission.

Philanthropy is the place these all come together. It serves both the needs of those who utilize the services of a nonprofit organization and the needs of supporters to express their purpose and passions. Understanding and operating out of this perspective can tremendously elevate the value of both the work of the nonprofit organization and the role of the donor to the organization. You cannot have one without the other.

When nonprofits consider donors or volunteers as merely a commodity, the donor may feel as if they are only being used for financial resources. The relationship will feel transactional and one-sided, which is not really a relationship at all. Non-relational transactions sabotage both the organization and the cause for which they are working, ultimately making an investment in the nonprofit a bad fit for most donors.

On the contrary, if nonprofits focus on building relationships around a common cause and on developing people to carry the cause forward, a donor's desire to give naturally follows.

Money is only one piece of the value exchanged. An organization relationally focused offers the donor an avenue for their values to be expressed and a place for their passions to come to life. Giving to meet the needs of such an organization is a meaningful and rewarding process as relationships like these are built over time.

You might ask, "This sounds nice in theory, but does this philosophy actually work for real nonprofits?" This philosophy has been developed through years of extensive experience, study and learning in the charitable sector and through formal education and research. My colleagues include faculty members at the IU Center and School of Philanthropy, School of Public and Environmental Affairs and The Fund Raising School. I have trained tens of thousands of people from over 30 countries on the various topics of philanthropy and the nonprofit sector. Repeatedly and consistently, it has been proven relationships are the key to healthy organizations, strong donor support, and impact.

The Three Pillars

As we said earlier, we have unfortunately become conditioned to only think of philanthropy in terms of money. However, the core of true philanthropy is expressed in society in three voluntary expressions of love for people.

We call these the three pillars of true philanthropy:

1. ***Giving:*** *The act of sharing your resources.*
2. ***Volunteering:*** *Freely giving your own time and giftedness/talents to a cause.*
3. ***Advocacy:*** *Championing something you value as much or more than yourself, connecting others to the cause and coming alongside those for which you care.*

When you are able to engage in all three pillars of philanthropy, you will find philanthropy to be more than writing a check. Your gifts and involvement will have increased meaning, fulfillment and impact.

We will examine nonprofits and the three pillars at a deeper level later in the book, but this simple overview gives you what you need to get started on your journey of giving for impact.

[icon] + NPO + [icons] = *Impact*

CHAPTER 2

WHY IMPACT MATTERS

Impact matters because simply doing good work does not equal changed lives.

Unfortunately, not all help actually helps. Some well-intended help even hurts those we serve.

A director of a nonprofit, who fed and clothed those in poverty, was approached by a dear lady she had seen many times before receiving their services. The woman smiled and said proudly, "I've been coming here for years and today my granddaughter is here to become a 'customer' too." The director greeted the young woman, but that day something clicked. The director thought, "Repeat 'customers' isn't our goal!" They had watched their numbers served increase over the past few years and had even celebrated in their newsletters how many more they were reaching with their services. Their donors were thrilled they could help more people. But that day she had been faced with the reality they may have been measuring the wrong things and asking the wrong questions.

The heart of their mission was not to see more people in poverty receiving their services but rather to help them move out of their circumstances. The organization began to research factors that contributed to poverty. These factors included mental health concerns, lack of knowledge about budgeting money, unhealthy personal relationships, lack of healthcare and substance abuse. The nonprofit also discovered the unpleasant truth that some of their "handout" services, instead of helping people move out of poverty, actually kept them in poverty by creating a dependency upon these services. The organizatoin realized major changes were needed.

Impact matters because simply doing good work does not equal changed lives. Understanding impact, and your role in it, can significantly affect a cause and the people it serves.

As we explore the idea of giving for impact, we are looking for the right fit that allows you to make the most impact toward the cause(s) you believe in. Because all partnerships are not equal, all work is not equal and all results are not equal.

You will learn to navigate what types of efforts produce certain kinds of impact. You will also learn what types of service create impact that is difficult to define. And you will learn which types of nonprofits operate in ways that are the best fit for you to make an impact as a partner.

Vision: The 99% Rule

To make an impact, you must know where you are going and what you are doing. One of the greatest ways to accomplish this is by following the 99% rule. This rule came from John D. Rockefeller, who, no matter what you think about him or his values, was an organizational genius.

Rockefeller's philosophy was a strong organization consisted of two things:

1. *1% vision*
2. *99% of all the organization's resources aligned to focus on that vision*

Vision is the destination. Vision is different than the mission. The mission is the organization's core belief and actions taken to bring that belief to life. The vision is the destination to which the core belief and those actions are pointing.

For example, let's say your family or friends are taking a week-long vacation to the Grand Canyon. Your mission is a road trip. Your vision is the Grand Canyon.

Or your mission may be investing in the lives of kids in a specific neighborhood for their entire childhood. Your vision is a neighborhood where all kids graduate high school and move on to a career.

The Cat Coalition's mission is rescuing stray cats and educating people on how to care for them. Their vision is a community where all cats are healthy and well-cared for.

Rockefeller believed the vision had to be so strong and clear that it worked like gravity, pulling the rest of the organization to it. When it works correctly, there are exponential results which come from living out that 1% focus and clarity.

However, when the vision is not strong or clear, then the organization ends up with multiple "visions" pulling itself in opposite and competing directions.

If, along your road trip to the Grand Canyon, your family members or friends each decide they want to go somewhere else, you are not going to make it to the Grand Canyon. You will also end up with arguments about where you are going. One might say it sounds more fun to visit the mountains of Colorado on the way. Another might want to keep on going and head all the way to the beach. You will end up missing the point (vision) of the trip—the Grand Canyon.

If, while pursuing a neighborhood where kids graduate and step into careers, a team member with a heart for clothing starts a clothing bank to serve other people in the neighborhood, then resources that were meant for the kids are now diverted to the clothing bank. A clothing bank can be good, but you'll miss the point (vision) of your organization—kids graduating.

Aligned:

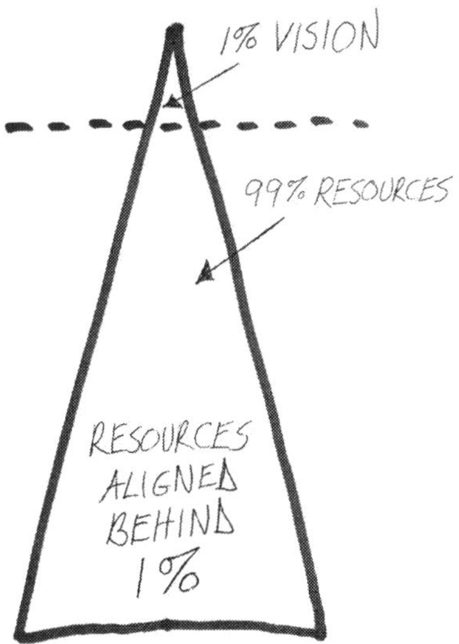

Misaligned:

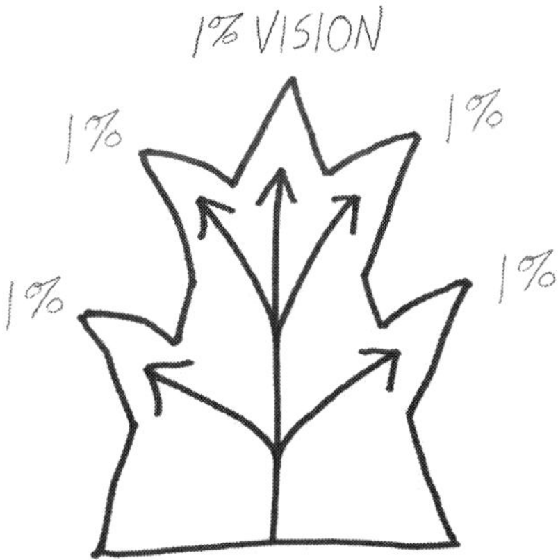

$$+ NPO + = Impact$$

Outputs And Outcomes

When a need is identified in society and a nonprofit is created, the nonprofit typically begins with some kind of activity to meet that need. The reason nonprofits start there is because it typically feels good to jump in and help. Eventually we find helping, does not really help.

For example, if the need is hunger, then we give meals. We answer the need (hunger) with an activity (meals). We then track those activities and call the numbers "outputs."

Outputs are things like:

- *How many people were served*
- *How many students went through the program*
- *How many meals were given away*

The goal of these outputs is to create some kind of change. This change is called an "outcome."

Outcomes are things like:

- *Moving to self-sufficiency*
- *Moving from addiction to sobriety*
- *At-risk youth graduating high school*

The activity leads to the output (numbers), which leads to the outcome (change).

Activity → Output → Outcome
(Actions → Numbers → Change)

If there are multiple outcomes, then a nonprofit might collect these outcomes and call it "impact." Impact representing the sum total of the outcomes. Impact which will then be used to define the vision.

For example, the Cat Coalition saw a need (malnourished and homeless cats) and created activities (stray cat rescue and cat care education). The organization measured how many strays were rescued and how many people attended educational workshops (outputs). Through the stray rescue and educational workshops, the organization discovered cats were gaining weight, eating a healthier diet and given safer shelter than before (outcomes). The Cat Coalition celebrated these outcomes with a press release sharing the collective impact. Soon after, in the second year of their organization, they began crafting a vision statement that focused on helping cats gain weight, eat healthy food and live in safe shelter.

If we follow this typical pathway, it would look something like this:

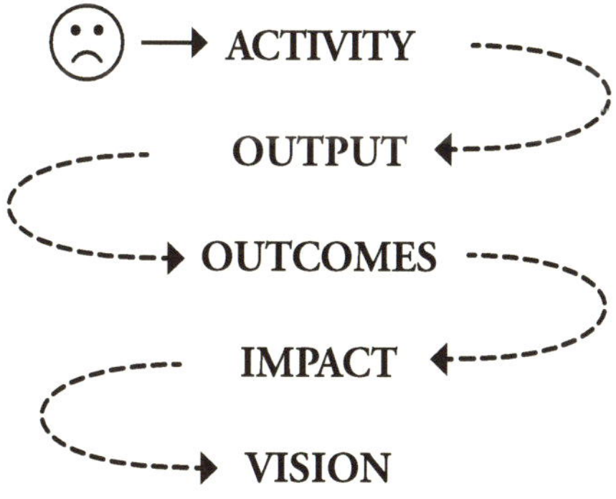

1. See the need
2. Create an activity to meet that need
3. Measure activity (output)
4. Define what change happened as a result of the output (outcome)
5. Collect the outcomes to define the impact
6. Use the impact to define the organization's vision

Well-intentioned people see a need, jump in and create activities, these services are measured in some type of output, those services and outputs creates a change, that change then creates an impact, and that impact is what we use to justify our vision.

While this is often what happens with nonprofit organizations, do you see something wrong with this plan?

It's upside-down.

The activity is driving the organization, not the vision.

We should not only address the need, we need to understand why that need exists in the first place. We need to understand the context of the need which is what helps us define the vision. We end up addressing symptoms not the root problem (destination).

If there are starving, malnourished cats running around exposed to the elements, why are they starved and malnourished in the first place? What factors are keeping cats from healthy food and safe shelter?

+ NPO + = Impact

For example, people saw kids who were hungry and wanted to help. Which is fantastic. They got together and decided one of the simplest ways to help these kids is to send food home with them in backpacks. However, they later discovered kids who went home with these backpacks were being abused and the food was being sold for drugs and sex. Parents were angered at the kids because they felt their poverty was exposed and they were taking handouts. Siblings targeted other siblings because they brought food home from school.

Does that mean the backpack is wrong? No, but trying to address a need without knowing why the need exists, or understanding the context, or the best way to intervene is a problem.

This happens on a small scale. It also happens on a global scale.

For example, a large global foundation invested over a billion dollars in their international initiatives over a 10-year period. When the impact evaluations were done, they discovered it failed to move the needle on true impact. In many cases, they actually created more social ills than existed prior to their funding. In some communities in Africa, where organizations spent decades restoring community through agriculture, micro-business, sanitation and water, the evaluations found communities to be in worse shape than they were 20 years before. Those in the community will have to spend another 20 years working to salvage the progress the foundation dismantled in their well-intentioned grant-making programs. This initiative failed because the vision was defined by what people said they should be doing (activities and outputs) without understanding the true need or context and what the real destination should be.

If you want to address needs in Africa or want to send backpacks of food home with kids or want to rescue cats, you absolutely can. You simply need to do it through an organization or a process that understands the context of the need and knows how to address it in a way that is going to result in positive change.

I do not say this to throw stones at these well-meaning efforts. I want us, instead, to see how critical it is to understand the need and then use that understanding to identify what organizations have a vision defined around that need. To not operate on what feels good, but rather ensure we know what will create meaningful change.

If we understand the need, we can define what life can look like if that need is addressed. From there, we can more effectively define the impact we are trying to create. After that, we can decide what outcomes are needed to achieve that impact. Those outcomes can then determine what outputs are needed. Then, those outputs can define our daily activities.

Therefore, instead of this typical nonprofit path:

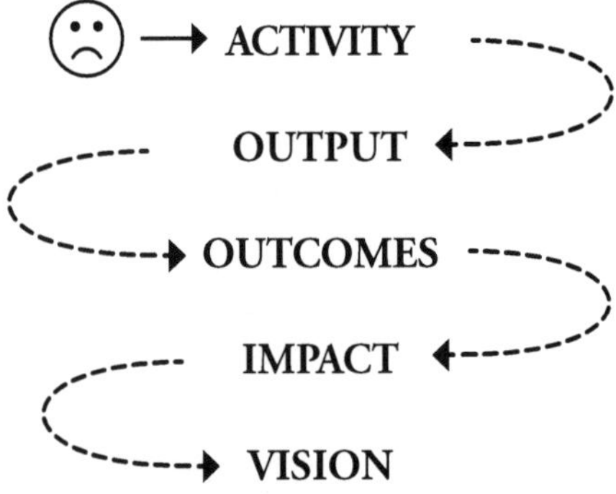

1. See the need

2. Create an activity to meet that need

3. Measure that activity (output)

4. Define what change happened as a result of the output (outcome)

5. Collect the outcomes to define the impact

6. Use the impact to define the organization's vision

It would ideally look like:

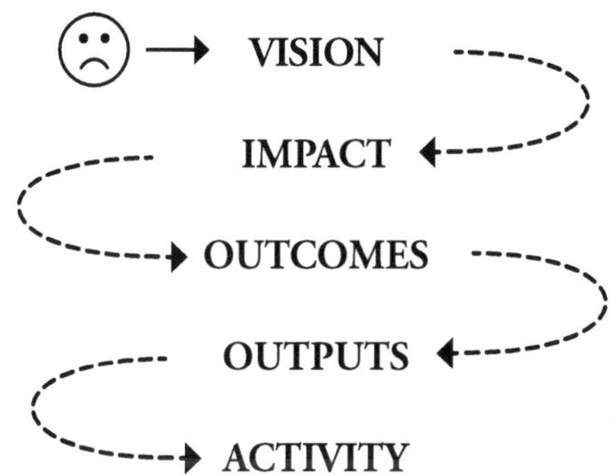

1. See the need

2. Understand the need (and context)

3. Use the understanding to define the vision of the organization

4. Use the vision to define the impact

5. Use the impact to define the outcomes

6. Use the outcomes to define the outputs

7. Use the outputs to define the activities

Let's reverse our previous example. What if the Cat Coalition saw the need (malnourished and homeless cats) and instead of starting an activity, worked to understand the need. Their research led them to conclude the major cause behind malnourished and homeless cats was actually cat owners abandoning their cat's kittens. This population of kittens (growing at a rate of 130 per year) were dropped off a few miles away to fend for themselves without care.

Therefore, they decided to serve malnourished and homeless cats by reversing kitten abandonment. They helped abandoned kittens find good homes (understanding defined the vision). They worked to connect as many kittens as possible to loving homes (vision defined impact). In the first year alone, not only were there fewer malnourished and homeless cats as the previous year, but kittens were being connected to safe homes (outcomes). They measured the dwindling homeless cat population and the number of kittens connected to homes (outputs). They did this by creating a stray kitten shelter where cat owners could drop off unwanted kittens, by creating a kitten rescue team who searched for abandoned kittens each week, and by promoting their services in the community (activities).

Donors Can Influence Impact

This is a major issue in the world of nonprofits, especially those with major funders. For example, I have worked with many organizations operating under federal grants. In these grants, the government has dictated, "The way you address this specific need is by doing this specific activity, so we want you to do and measure this specific activity." The nonprofit is funded by them and therefore does this activity, yet many times evaluations are showing this activity is not creating change. The actual value being created by the organization is something no one is tracking because they do not have a funder telling them it matters.

The Cat Coalition could be tracking attendance at cat care education workshops, but not know if cat care education makes any difference in helping cats become healthier and safer. What if the main problem causing unhealthy and homeless cats is completely unrelated to education?

When we respond first at an emotional level, it does not mean our activities do not actually help. But it does mean it is a guessing game as to whether or not it helps...or even hurts. While giving makes me feel good as a donor, at some point, we will begin to question if we are truly making a difference.

Let's say a survey showed depression was a growing issue in your community. What if a group of people got together to address this issue. One prominent member of the group said, "You know what cheers people up? A high five! What if we helped people by giving them high fives?" The group thought this sounded like a fun and simple way to encourage people. So they created a goal to give out 1,000,000 high fives during the next year. It went viral locally, with people posting videos of high fives, making fun T-shirts and creating high-five meetups. They reached their goal within just six months.

However, studies came out the next year showing depression was an even greater issue than before. The high fives were successful in their goals but made no impact on the issue of depression. Their vision of 1,000,000 high fives did not understand the need or context of depression. It was based on their activities and outputs.

You, as a donor, have a unique opportunity to ask questions and to speak into the organization regarding these issues. I have personally been part of numerous situations where a donor was bold enough to ask hard questions. Questions about impact, why they do what they do and what is the real outcome of their service. These questions, combined with insight from the donor, actually led the organization to new insights that caused them to review and refine how they approached measuring impact in a low-income constituency they serve. The donors insights led to a new approach and ultimately to new funding as well. These donors influenced impact.

Impact Pathway

When a nonprofit understands the larger picture and their role within it, they can create an impact pathway. This impact pathway is an illustration showing the need, the vision and their role within the larger picture of restoration. It aids the nonprofit in defining outcomes, outputs and activities that fit their organization and those that do not. The pathway even helps clarify which types of funding fit their organization and which do not.

An impact pathway gives clarity for every area of the organization. It serves as a guide leading them clearly toward their vision.

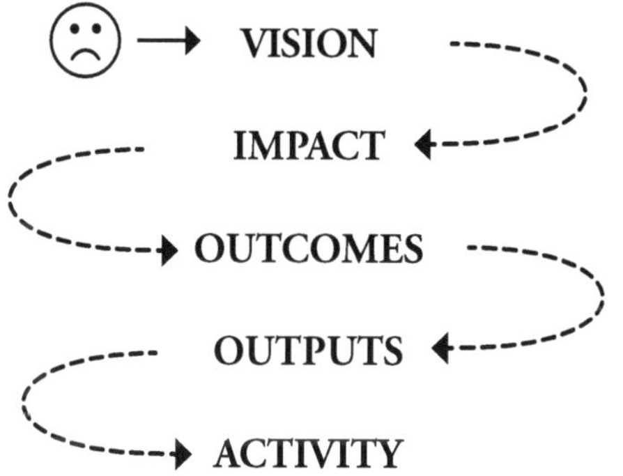

The Three R's

On the impact pathway, there are three types of services, which we call the three R's:

1. *Relief*
2. *Rehab*
3. *Restoration*

Understanding the differences between these types of services, as well as where and how an organization fits into the three R's, is a major aid to finding the right nonprofit with which to partner.

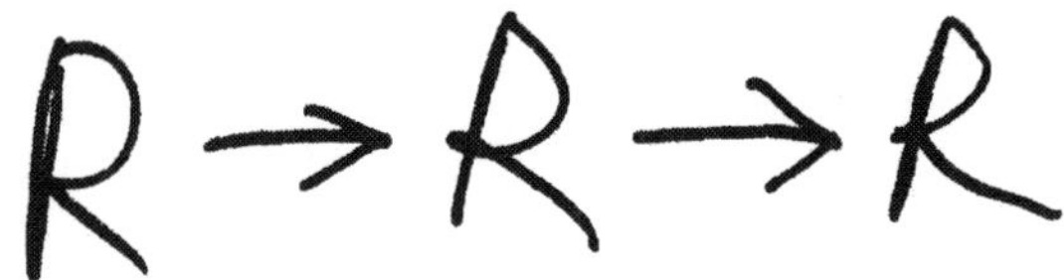

Relief

For example, if you are working with an organization to mentor at-risk kids in a specific neighborhood, relief is providing an immediate safe place after school. After school is a high-risk time for kids in an urban environment and many are in need of food. Relief work provides these kids a safe place to go.

The nonprofit is intervening with immediate relief. Before someone is able to be helped forward toward the next phase (rehab), they need to have their immediate needs met.

Rehab

Because the relief work has addressed the immediate issues of safety and food, the nonprofit is then able to begin the rehab work of serving the children. If the nonprofit discovers one specific child struggles with reading, they are now in a position to begin helping them work on that.

Rehab helps provide stabilization. At this level, understanding is built on why someone is in need and the nonprofit is working to help the person move forward.

Restoration

Restoration is then understanding the need and context deeply enough to discover root causes that created the need for relief in the first place. If you want to see the children in this neighborhood with fewer needs for relief, you need to be able to address the root causes that created the need. If parents' drug problems are the root issue, you can then begin addressing that. If it is something else, or a combination of things, you can begin addressing those things.

The ideal restoration would be to do such a good job addressing root causes and issues as a nonprofit that you ultimately put yourself out of business.

If a nonprofit is successful at restoration, their success will often reduce the need for relief.

If a nonprofit is successful at restoration in mentoring the at-risk kids, then at some point kids in the neighborhood will find new opportunities for positive growth. They will find positive ways to impact their homes and their neighborhood. They will graduate high school, and maybe even beyond, and become contributors to their neighborhood. The nonprofit will begin to see improved quality of life for these individuals with less need for food and safety. They will be addressing and impacting the root causes of those issues.

It is the opposite of what happened with the global foundation we discussed earlier where the "success" of their relief work led to a need for more relief work. The success of restoration work should lead to less relief work.

Continuum

Let's be honest, whether addressed on your own, or even with an organization, the size and complexity of many problems cause issues to appear truly impossible to solve.

This is why at least doing something, like sending backpacks with food home with a child, seems like an opportunity to take part in a small way. If you cannot even begin to address the full problem, doing some kind of activity gives you a place to start, right? We reason it may feel like fighting a forest fire with a cup of water, but it is at least something.

However, let's look at this from a larger level.

Shepherd Community Center in Indianapolis is considered a national model for urban poverty intervention. Their unique impact pathway limits them to serving 500 families or less. They have a 25-year continuum, serving kids and youth, in statistically one of roughest neighborhoods in Indianapolis. Kids enter their programs around age five. Shepherd stays with them until they graduate from a college or vocational program and are back impacting the neighborhood. Their focus is equipping people to be change-makers long-term for this neighborhood.

Shepherd provides specific services as an organization, including education, food and even a unique police/first responder service. But, even in their 25-year continuum with hundreds of families, there is simply no way they would be able to provide everything those families need. Shepherd knows the concerns with which they should specifically intervene, but they also know who else needs to intervene with them over those 25 years. They can map out where every person and every organization needs to fit in the continuum to drive restoration of that specific neighborhood.

We cannot do everything, neither as an individual nor a single organization.

Therefore, we each need to understand where we fit in the context of the three R's as well as in the context of others working to help the same people in different ways. Where we complement one another instead of compete.

Ultimately, philanthropy should lead toward restoration. Even organizations focused on relief play a role that should ultimately help lead to restoration. Otherwise we are creating services that are not creating transformation and may even be creating dependency. Like we covered earlier, successful restoration work should lead to less relief work. If all nonprofits ultimately point to restoration as the goal, then they understand their services (whether relief, rehab or restoration) are a stop on the journey to restoration.

If you are a cat lover considering getting involved with the Cat Coalition, you can ask them how their work fits in relief, in rehab and in restoration. The Cat Coalition does some work in all three but focuses most of its efforts on rescuing strays. Therefore, their work fits primarily in relief.

And that is okay if they understand the context of their organization. If they understand how they serve in the relief area and how other animal services address rehab and restoration, then the Cat Coalition plays a role in the larger issue of cat restoration, a world where cat populations are controlled and cats are loved and cared for appropriately.

When we see ourselves and the organizations we partner with as specific steps along the larger journey toward restoration, we can better understand our role in the causes we care about. Even for problems that seem too large to address, we can begin to see how our "cup" of water fighting the forest fire is joining hundreds or thousands of others working on the same problem. You may only be able to do one little piece, but that piece is needed and fits within the broader picture or continuum of care.

You are part of the total impact. You are part of restoration.

A Deeper Look At The Three R's

As a donor, understanding the three R's helps you know:

1. *Where an organization fits on the continuum (or if they even know)*
2. *Where you fit on the continuum*

When an organization knows where it fits on the continuum, they should be able to show you the bigger picture of restoration and their place in that. They should be able to show how they interact with other organizations to better serve their clients and address the larger cause.

The Cat Coalition should be able to show you how their stray rescue services fit within the larger cause of cat restoration.

In the same way, you as a donor may be drawn toward a specific fit within the three R's. When you know where you fit and what you have a passion to impact, you can more clearly know what kinds of organizations you should partner with.

As we discussed with the impact pathway, when an organization is clear on its vision to the point of understanding where it fits on the continuum of care, they can articulate how they contribute to the larger picture. They can help you as a donor understand their impact within the larger picture. Clearly understanding this also helps them stay true to their vision and then invite the right donors to come along.

$$\text{🐱} + NPO + \text{👥} = Impact$$

Big Numbers Don't Always Mean Big Results

As you move from relief toward restorative work on the continuum of care, number of people served begins to decrease. In our culture, many people are easily impressed by big numbers. However, big numbers do not always mean big results. When you as a donor can understand why an organization serves 30 kids instead of 3,000, you can clearly understand whether or not you would be good partners.

From an organization standpoint, if it has not articulated or translated the impact of serving those 30 kids instead of 3,000, then you as a donor cannot understand why investing so deeply in those 30 kids matters. Donors are often left with what feels good or meaningful. If you fully understand the impact, it might feel meaningful to invest in those 30 kids. But if you do not know why, if you do not truly understand the impact, then it often feels more meaningful to invest in a cause serving larger numbers of the population. This is a critical concept we will explore more deeply later in the book.

If both donors and organizations are educated about the three R's and understand their roles in the larger continuum, they can become better partners and make more of an impact for the cause, allowing everyone to win.

Characteristics Of The Three R's

Organizations that focus on different areas of the three R's often look very different from one another, both internally and externally.

For example, evaluation in a relief organization is going to look dramatically different, and far more cost effective, than evaluation in a restoration project. As a donor, you need to know that and know why.

In the same way, scale and growth in a relief organization is going to look remarkably different than restoration.

What you value as a donor will impact which type of organization you partner with. Understanding yourself will also help you understand how you relate to the cause. For example, with the issue of poverty. Your life experiences and worldview will cause you to relate to a child in poverty very differently than another person might.

A few donors were talking about helping with a Christmas toy outreach. They shared what the kids, who were living in what we would consider poverty, wanted for Christmas. These middle-school students' list included things like an Xbox, Nintendo, iPhone, etc. All normal things you would expect a middle-school student to want.

One of the ladies said, "I cannot believe the audacity of these kids."

She could not believe the kids would ask for entertainment and luxuries because they were in poverty.

+ NPO + = Impact

What do you think she was reacting to?

She was expressing a bias that said, "These kids are in poverty. How dare they ask for an iPhone. They should be asking for things that kids in poverty should be asking for. Can you believe this is on their Christmas list?"

I guess not everyone wants government cheese for Christmas.

This woman had a relationship to poverty that caused her to project a bias that somehow if you are in poverty as a kid, you cannot dream anymore. That you cannot want the things normal American kids would want.

This is a real issue regarding our biases and baggage on how we relate to any topic. Because that is the case with every issue. People are messy.

If you see kids in poverty as needing practical Christmas gifts instead of normal, fun presents, then a Christmas toy outreach probably is not your best fit.

As a donor, you need to ask yourself, "How do I relate to this issue?" It is more than asking, "Do I have a passion for this issue?" It is understanding your fit. It is understanding what underlying thoughts and assumptions you bring to the issue.

MY GUIDEPOINTS FOR THE THREE R's OF SCALABILITY			
GUIDE POINT	**RELIEF**	**REHAB**	**RESTORATION**
Collaboration	*Low*	*Moderate*	*High*
Engagement	*Easier*	*Moderate*	*Harder*
Scale	*Linear*	*Compounding*	*Exponential*
Numbers Served	*High*	*Moderate*	*Lower*
Relationship to Those Served	*Transactional*	*Growing*	*Intimate and Complex*
Timeline of Change	*Months*	*Years*	*Multiple Years*
Impact	*Shorter Term*	*Moderate*	*Longitudinal*
Measures of Change	*Easy*	*Moderate*	*Difficult*
Change Process	*Clear*	*Moderate*	*Complex*
Instant Gratification	*High*	*Moderate*	*Low*
Difficulty to Raise $	*Low*	*Moderate*	*High*
Equipping/ Education	*Easy*	*Moderate*	*Difficult*
Skill	*Logistical*	*Increasing Relational*	*High Relational*
Staff Concentration	*Limited*	*Increasing Relational*	*Heavy*
Efficiency	*High*	*Moderate*	*Low*
Cost of Change (Admin Ratios)	*Low*	*Moderate*	*High*

MY FIT IN THE THREE R's			
GUIDE POINT	RELIEF	REHAB	RESTORATION
Collaboration			
Engagement			
Scale			
Numbers Served			
Relationship to Those Served			
Timeline of Change			
Impact			
Measures of Change			
Change Process			
Instant Gratification			
Difficulty to Raise $			
Equipping/ Education			
Skill			
Staff Concentration			
Efficiency			
Cost of Change (Admin Ratios)			

Rate the type of giving you prefer by placing an X in one of the Three R categories (Relief, Rehab, or Restoration) for each guide point.

MEANINGFUL GIVING

Philanthropy is an opportunity to engage your heart, mind and soul in the deepest ways possible and therefore discover meaning and fulfillment in your giving.

As you find your fit in philanthropy, you will not only make more impact through your giving, you will also begin to discover more meaning.

Giving "token" gifts out of obligation or by default will not engage you deeply enough to find meaning in your involvement with a cause. Philanthropy is an opportunity to engage your heart, mind and soul in the deepest ways possible and therefore discover meaning and fulfillment in your giving. The most fulfilled donors I get to work with are those who have found ways to incorporate all three of these elements. They find fulfillment in the difference they know they are making in society.

$$+ NPO + \quad = Impact$$

TOKEN vs. FULFILLED GIVING

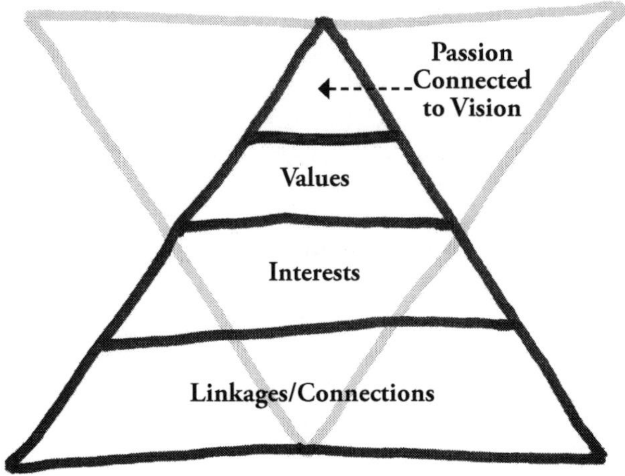

The graphic above shows how fulfillment increases as you find your fit at the top of the pyramid. Unfortunately, most give at the bottom and never experience the meaning that is possible by finding their fit.

Finding Yourself

How do you move toward the top of this pyramid? You must be willing to take the time to become a student of yourself. You cannot figure out the right fit or the right partners until you first know yourself.

Understanding Vision and Passion

Knowing yourself means knowing your personal vision for making a difference in the world and what experiences and values in your life drive the passion behind that vison.

Why?

Why does this matter?

We are each wired to love people in unique ways. You have a combination of abilities, interests, values, resources, passions and connections that no one else has. When you move toward the right fit and "outlet" for these things, your giving experience will be energized. You begin to discover the joy and fulfillment giving can provide. The more engaged your heart and mind are around a cause, the more impact and sacrificial giving you will want to make. Your giving will become more of a true reflection of yourself.

Giving is a deep, personal inner choice. Far more than writing a check, it includes your time, your resources and your heart. Therefore, when nonprofits resort to transactional practices instead of relational ones, they rob you of the chance to experience this joy and fulfillment.

We all have a desire to be known and to be in relationships that are more than transactional. I work with recording artists in Nashville to help them navigate the concerns in developing fulfilling relationships in an industry where it is so easy to feel seen only for their money and their name. These artists desire opportunities to be involved with causes they have a passion to impact in unique and meaningful ways. Without these opportunities they tell me, "I feel like a commodity to them." So it is for the relationships between us as a donor and a nonprofit. When interactions are reduced to merely securing a donor's name on the bottom of a check, the exchange is commodified and the value of the relationship is undermined.

This should not be so.

Being a commodity in someone else's plan is not your best fit to love people. Do not settle for a mediocre relationship. Do not settle for mediocre giving. Do not settle for inferior impact.

Instead, you have the opportunity to develop a strong relationship as you bond over a shared cause. It is a community of people coming together.

+ NPO + = Impact

A mother's sacrificial love for her baby creates a unique bond that does not compare to other relationships. This connection cannot be found outside of the sacrifices (giving) that the mother makes. In a similar way, giving (and the sacrifices involved) with an organization can create a bond of relationship that cannot be found any other way.

Giving is expressed in relationship.

Within these kinds of relationships, you can make an impact no matter your bank account, no matter your skills and no matter your abilities.

You can build relationships around a cause. You can help move the cause forward. You can find a meaningful fit in giving. You can influence an organization and therefore influence the work and cause.

You can create change.

+ NPO + = Impact

CHAPTER 4

IMPACTFUL GIVING

Your ability to create change can grow and deepen as you find your unique fit in philanthropy.

Now that you have a strong foundation to understand what giving for impact looks like, you are ready to start your journey through the giving for impact equation.

**KNOW YOURSELF
+ KNOW THE ORGANIZATION
+ KNOW WHAT PARTNERSHIP LOOKS LIKE
= MEANINGFUL IMPACT**

Let's look a little more deeply at this equation for developing a clearer understanding of your fit in philanthropy.

We have established you can create change and your ability to take part in this impact equation allows you to make a difference in a cause(s) you care for.

If philanthropy is how you express your love for people, and if nonprofits serve to connect you to people and cause(s) you have a passion for, then the goal you are working toward is to find and develop partnerships that create change.

Partnerships are formed because both sides provide value, as we said before. You as a donor, volunteer and advocate represent one of those sides, and you have value to offer.

Your value in a partnership with an organization is not based on the dollar amount of your donation. Your value to the cause, and ability to create change, is because of your relationship. Together, both sides create a multiplied impact.

It is important to understand this because it is easy to dismiss our value as individual donors and assume corporations, foundations and the wealthy are the primary drivers of philanthropy.

Out of the hundreds of billions of dollars given to charities each year, do you know what percentage is donated by corporations?

5%.

And when we factor in bequests – which come from individuals, and giving from family foundations and trusts, we end up with nearly 88% of charitable giving in the United States coming from individuals like you and I.*

In fact, current estimates show us giving is more of a bell curve. Some estimates place that about half of giving comes from households making approximately $110,000 or less per year. Everyday people coming together for change creates impact.

Your ability to create change can grow and deepen, not only if or when your donations or volunteer time increase, but as you find your unique fit in philanthropy.

** Individual giving is comprised of all direct individual giving, planned giving (individuals) and family foundations (comprised of individual families as opposed to independent grantmaking foundations).*

We are each wired with unique gifts, abilities, values and passions that can help make the world around us a better place. As we move closer and closer to our unique fit, our ability to create change will grow.

How do you discover your fit?

Through the equation for impact:

1. *Know yourself*
2. *Know nonprofit organizations*
3. *Know how to build healthy partnerships/relationships with nonprofits*

The more you are able to understand these, the more you will be able to discover your fit.

CHAPTER 5

KNOW YOURSELF

The first step in finding your fit in philanthropy is to better understand yourself.

Like we said earlier, knowing yourself is the first step. Finding your fit in philanthropy is not simply finding a mission for giving but finding a mission for life. It is a vision for life through which your giving is reflected. It is discovering your unique purpose or calling. It informs how you live and how you give. Think of it as a core component to your personal mission statement.

The first step in finding your fit is to better understand yourself. What do you want to accomplish? What do you dream about changing? How do you believe is the best way to go about that work? This section will equip you to better answer those questions. Your answers will then help clarify what kind of partnerships to look for.

Remember our discussion about meaningful giving. Your fulfillment increases as you move up the pyramid. When your fulfillment increases, so does your impact.

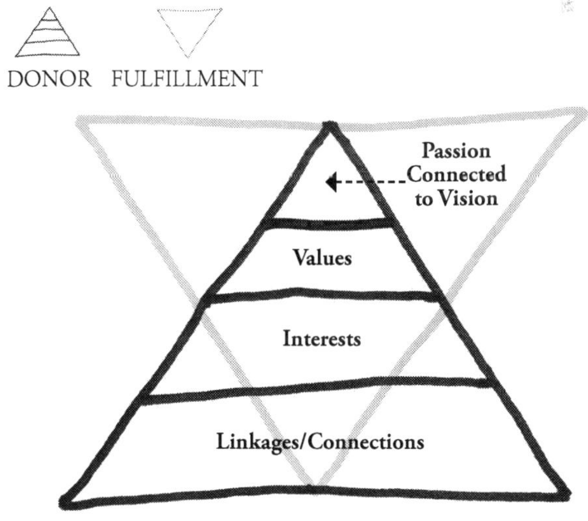

Linkage, Interests, Values and Passion

There are four main factors to consider when discovering your fit:

1. *Linkage (connections)*
2. *Interests*
3. *Values*
4. *Passion connected to Vision*

These factors are not "paperwork" designed to arbitrarily manufacture a mission or vision. Consider them guides to help you build relationships and partnerships.

Let's take a few minutes to define these four factors.

Linkage:

Linkage is simply who or what you are connected to. You are connected to the people you know, the businesses you drive by, the people and organizations you learn about online, the groups you are a part of.

You cannot know about a cause or organization unless you have learned about it through someone or something. This is an obvious statement, but if you step into the shoes of an organization, this is where they must start. They have a responsibility to create some kind of link or connection to even make people aware they exist. They must find a path to your door.

What things do you have interest in and linkage to?
(e.g. families and parenting, seniors and health, cats and collars?)

____

____

____

____

____

____

____

Interests:

You can be "linked" or connected to very many things you have no interest in. You are linked simply by seeing their billboard on your way to work, your co-worker's daughter does a fundraiser each year or you saw someone share it online. Being friends with someone who leads an Ostrich Farm Think Tank does not mean you are involved in any way or that you have any potential interest in it. You are simply connected.

Questions like these can help you uncover the types of causes and work you have an interest in:

- *What are you interested in?*
- *What peaks your curiosity?*
- *What do you find yourself wanting to learn more about?*
- *What do you enjoy talking about?*

Interest is different than simply believing in a cause. Many causes and charitable works do very good things many of us believe in. However, there may be a few certain organizations you are specifically interested in learning about, talking about and getting involved in.

There is an unlimited supply of needs to be met, but a very limited supply of your own personal resources to give. This is true for every person, regardless of their abilities, status or wealth.

Therefore, discovering the causes you are most interested in helps lead you one step closer to finding your best fit in philanthropy.

What are you interested in?

____

____

What peaks your curiosity?

____

____

What do you find yourself wanting to learn more about?

____

____

What do you enjoy talking about?

____

____

+ NPO + = Impact

Values:

The next step after clarifying your interests is defining your values. Your values guide your decisions in everything from choosing what food to buy at the grocery store to choosing how to parent your children.

In the same way, uncovering and defining your values as they relate to your giving will provide you a clear picture of what types of work and organizations are a good fit. Understanding your values can help you more easily say no to the wrong things and yes to the right. It can keep you focused on creating the most meaningful impact you can for the cause(s) you love.

Core values are those things that determine how you will go about life, no matter what you do. They are the bedrock of how you approach all things in life, including your giving.

Write down what you see as your core values that drive how you live. *(e.g. integrity, faith, family, relationships, etc.)*

____

____

____

____

____

NPO + = Impact

Passion:

What do you have a longing to change?

Passion for a cause moves beyond intellectual curiosity and alignment with your values. It is something that pulls at your heart when you think about it. It moves you to want to take action. It may even keep you awake at night. It might feel like a calling.

It may be big, or it may be small. It may be general, or it may be incredibly specific.

When you engage in a cause you are passionate about instead of simply agreeing with, you are more likely to engage more deeply. You will more likely want to involve all three pillars (resources, time and heart). Giving at this deeper, more engaged level will make a greater impact on you, the organization and the cause.

What cause(s) most excites you? Why?
(What raises the hair on your arms when you think about doing something to make a difference in that area?)

____

____

____

____

____

Mission:

In addition to these four factors, understanding mission, vision and the 9 donor trade-offs (which will soon be addressed) are important components to knowing yourself.

Your mission is your core belief and how you intend to realize that core belief in your life. Your personal mission informs how you give. (From the earlier example, the mission is the road trip).

Write down what you see as your personal mission that informs how you give.

____

____

____

____

____

____

____

____

Vision:

Just like Rockefeller's 1% vision, your work with the four factors can help you determine the vision of what you want to see happen in the world. What impact are you wanting to make? What picture comes to your mind of what the future could become? Your vision is WHERE you want to go. (From the earlier example, the vision is the destination).

Finding your authentic vision and ordering your resources around it will help you to find your best fit in philanthropy, in loving people.

What impact are you wanting to make?
(What picture comes to your mind of what the future could become?)

____

____

____

____

____

____

____

____

9 Donor Trade-Offs:

As you discover your unique mission and vision, another key way to help understand your personal fit in philanthropy is discovering what values drive HOW you want to make a difference. There are nine major spectrums that define how work is done.[1] Your personality, experience, and perspective will affect where you fall on each spectrum. There are typically trade-offs associated with each side of each spectrum.

The tool on the next page shares the nine major spectrums of how work is done and allows you to visually chart your values on each spectrum. Your personal values will determine what trade-offs you will consider in your partnerships. This tool gives you a "map" of your personal giving philosophy. These results can help guide you as you explore potential nonprofit partnerships because you know more about who you are.

This tool can be used to help provide clarity for individuals, families and foundations. Some foundations use this exercise collectively and then afterward allow their individual board members to do the same thing. Those board members can see insights into their own dissonance with the foundation's grant-making. Things like, "Okay, when I feel resistance to a grant we are making, it is not because it is the wrong grant to make for the foundation. It is because my philosophy on one of these spectrums is different than the foundation's."

There is neither a right or wrong side on each spectrum, it simply helps people to understand how they are or are not congruent with others. If there is a disconnect, it will provide clarity on why someone might be feeling tension on a decision or out of alignment with others.

My Giving Philosophy

Put an X where you believe you are on the continuum:

Efficiency ____________ vs. ____________ **Effectiveness**

Focus ____________ vs. ____________ **Flexibility**

Capacity ____________ vs. ____________ **Capability**

Speed ____________ vs. ____________ **Thoroughness**

Solutions ____________ vs. ____________ **Systems**

Unique ____________ vs. ____________ **Standard**

Independent ____________ vs. ____________ **Collaborative**

Experiment ____________ vs. ____________ **Investment**

Leader ____________ vs. ____________ **Organization**

+ NPO + = *Impact*

1. *Efficiency vs. Effectiveness*

Do you value clear and highly efficient systems? If you give to something that is highly efficient, then it is most likely going to be relief type work in its nature. If you give to something that is more inefficient and complex, it is typically going to be more restorative. They are not mutually exclusive, but they are often in tension with one another. Knowing what you value helps you understand what types of efforts you want to support. Leaders in large corporations who work daily in quality management, operational efficiency, etc. may come into a neighborhood restoration project and have a false expectation that the neighborhood work should operate in the same way their manufacturing processes do. However, it does not work that way. We can create efficiency to a certain degree, but a major component of neighborhood restoration involves developing and redefining relationships. Building relationships will never be extremely efficient because they can be complex and messy.

2. Focus vs. Flexibility

Do you value specific focus on activities or the overall impact of the work?

For example, let's say you are supporting a restoration project focused on kids in a specific neighborhood graduating high school. Do you value funding programs that directly serve the child (e.g. tutoring, after-school program, etc.)? Or, if research shows the most pivotal factor in these kids graduating is equipping their grandparents, would you value investing in a grandparent program because it will ultimately provide more of an impact to the kids?

Focus means you would choose to restrict funds to those child-focused areas because they are what resonate with you. Flexibility means you have clarity on the type of big-picture impact you want to create and are willing to support any ways that best create the impact.

3. Capacity vs. Capability

Do you value impact by seeing more numbers served or by deepening the ability to create change? This comes back to our discussions about scale, growth and impact. Sometimes organizations can have both great capacity (numbers) and great capability (depth of impact), but there is often a trade-off. By definition, Shepherd's model of serving 500 or 1,000 families does not allow them to multiply their capacity. They could not partner with the donor who wanted them to serve 4,000 families. Restoration organizations do not often work in a model that can be taken to greater capacity by just serving more people. They cannot be multiplied in the same way that relief natured programs can. Their growth of impact comes by either transplanting that model to somewhere new or by investing more deeply in those they serve.

This can be a major tension point for donors. A donor who owns restaurant franchises and continues opening as many as possible may find it difficult to connect with a restoration project's focus on going deeper in capability instead of wider in capacity.

On the opposite side, a donor who works as a therapist may struggle to connect with a relief organization whose focus is serving high numbers of people but lacks opportunities for relational depth.

4. *Speed vs. Thoroughness*

Do you value speed over thoroughness? Speed is often connected to relief work, while thoroughness is often connected to restoration. For example, if a natural disaster like a hurricane hits, there is an immediate need for relief help of food, clothing and shelter. Yet, if you look at places where major hurricanes struck in the past decade, some are facing major long-term restoration needs that could not have been addressed by relief work. There are needs no one had dealt with before that are now wreaking havoc in those communities. This work would require the thoroughness of long-term restoration work.

Again, both are needed. Both are valuable. However, you may resonate with one more than the other.

5. Solutions vs. Systems

Are you an idea person or an implementation person?

Organizations that lean on the idea side are focused on finding innovative solutions to problems. Those that lean on the system side are focused on developing systems through which a solution can become sustainable.

Like the other trade-offs, an organization can be anywhere along the spectrum, but knowing where both you and the organization line up helps you to determine if you are a potential fit.

6. Unique vs. Standard

Do you like the "shiny and new" feel from your giving or do you like maximizing what you know works? Nonprofits often try to differentiate themselves by stressing what makes them unique.

Yet, sometimes the biggest impact can come from simply improving and growing an existing system that has been proven to work. Reinventing the wheel does not always result in the most impact.

You as a donor may lean toward unique perspectives and solutions, or you may lean toward supporting something that is already successfully making an impact.

$$\text{You} + NPO + \text{\$} = Impact$$

7. Independent vs. Collaborative

Do you like giving to organizations integrated with many other services or partners? Steve Jobs found working independently allowed him to test his ideas and bring them to market more quickly than waiting for a consensus. This approach works well for some organizations and resonates with like-minded donors.

Nevertheless, collaboration is critical for solving large-scale problems. Even a mammoth organization like the Gates Foundation does not have enough resources by itself to create a viable health system for West Africa.

There is typically a need for some kind of collaboration. However, the amount can vary from organization to organization and donor to donor. Charting where you and the organization are on this line can help you decide on a healthy partnership.

8. Experiment vs. Investment

Are you tolerant of failure? Some donors view their giving as an "investment" with a "social return-on-investment" in the same way they look to their 401(k) to provide a financial return-on-investment. In this model, donors are looking to maximize their investment with the highest impact that can be made with their donation.

On the flip side, some donors view their giving as an experiment where the organization is trying to learn and develop in order to discover the best solution to a problem. In this model, there is the possibility that a well-executed experiment ends up not working and loses money.

In the investment model, if I invest $1 million and do not see the expected impact, it is considered a failure. In the experiment model, failure to achieve the expected is simply seen as part of the process of learning, evaluating and refining how the organization addresses social change.

Thomas Edison, after thousands of unsuccessful attempts at the light bulb said, "I have not failed. I've just found 10,000 ways that won't work." This describes the mindset behind the experiment model. If you failed to hit your goal, but learned in the process, it is still considered success.

Your preference regarding this as a donor is a major factor to be considered. If you and the organization are not aligned on success and failure, it could have major negative consequences on your expectations and partnership.

+ NPO + = Impact

9. Leader vs. Organization

Do you find comfort in a strong leader or a strong organization? Is the organization focused around the leader or around the cause? From small to large, organizations can easily become persona-driven around a respected or charismatic leader.

You as a donor may intentionally or not intentionally connect with a leader instead of an organization. Whether through personal relationship, personality-driven communications or because of lack of trust in organizations themselves, it is easy to become person-focused instead of cause-focused.

While healthy organizations are not dependent upon one "superstar" leader, practicalities can easily cause some to lean more personality-driven than others. Ideally, even charismatic leaders are connecting people to the cause instead of to themselves. They should be building a high-capacity team and infrastructure around them to make an impact beyond themselves.

You as a donor need to understand what, or who, is motivating you to connect. And understand whether you believe the organization itself is trust-worthy, or if you are only trusting an individual. What happens to your support if the leader leaves? What happens to the organization if the leader leaves?

It can be tricky for both organizations and for donors, but it is an important issue to settle as you look for the right fit as a donor.

These trade-offs are tensions you need to be aware of as a donor. To navigate these, you should evaluate which ones are most important to you and how you see yourself in philanthropy. You can then determine which trade-offs you are willing to accept. Remember, you are not going to find a "perfect fit." You are building a relationship and finding the best fit, which includes compromise and trade-offs.

Your Fit In The Three R's

Let's return to the three R's - relief, rehab and restoration and the "My Fit In The Three R's" chart you filled out in Chapter Two. They each have different dynamics.

For example, if you want to scale or grow the impact of a relief-focused initiative, your results will most likely be larger or multiplied numbers. A food relief organization might say to the donor, "We're serving 500 people right now. Let's figure out how we can partner to serve 5,000." The underlying thought and assumption is that serving 5,000 people is both good and achievable.

At the opposite end of the spectrum, scaling or growing impact in a restoration-focused initiative looks dramatically different. Let's say a community development organization determined best practices to restore a neighborhood. So they may say to the donor, "We're serving one neighborhood right now. Let's partner to take this model to another neighborhood." This could be one community, one state or even one country over.

In the same way, increased impact for a restoration-focused initiative might involve doing even more intensive work with those whom they already serve. That same community development organization might say to a donor, "We're providing food security and career training services right now. We've discovered relational health is a major barrier for the residents in this neighborhood. Let's partner to begin providing relationship classes and coaching to these neighbors." Increased impact for these organizations is not the number of people or neighborhoods served, but instead deepening care for those already being served.

Like we said earlier, big numbers do not always mean big results. Do you see how different "growth" or "impact" can look for different organizations, depending on where they fit along the three R's? None of the organizations are "better" than the other, they simply have different focuses. Being clear on this and understanding your fit in this is key for a healthy partnership.

Sponsoring a child's food and clothing costs for $30 per month creates a different kind of impact (and costs less) than providing after-school tutoring, counseling, transportation and building a relationship with their families at a cost of $800 per month. The relief organization could say "invest in a child for only $30 per month" and they would be correct. However, the results of that impact are different than investing in restorative work for $800 per month. Neither is more "fiscally responsible" than the other. They are simply working to accomplish different things, which requires different investments.

Let's look at staffing a nonprofit. How will success in staffing look different for a relief-focused nonprofit compared to one focused on restoration?

Relief work requires a lot of people to distribute items like food or clothing. You want to increase the numbers of items, people, etc. It will be more transactional. Food drives, meal deliveries and clothing banks are all examples of this.

In contrast, restoration work requires deeper levels of skill for staffing and volunteers. They are going deeper instead of wider. It is going to be more relational. Examples of this would be Shepherd Community Center that we mentioned earlier, community development organizations and neighborhood-focused after-school programs.

$$\text{[icon]} + NPO + \text{[people icons]} = Impact$$

Measuring "change" with a relief model will look more straightforward and linear with things like numbers served, items distributed, etc. Change in a restoration model is going to be far more complex and dynamic because the change happens at a relational level. Restoration work is messy. It is much harder and more intensive to evaluate.

In other areas, the cost of services for relief work is far less expensive than restoration work. The timeline for change in relief work is much shorter than that of restoration. Relief work's administrative needs are much less than the more complex needs of restoration work.

Again, neither of these models is inherently "better" than another. They are simply working to accomplish different goals.

As a donor, you need to be very clear on what you value. Your preferences and fit with the nine donor trade-offs can help you clarify where you fit in the three R's. If you are passionate about productivity, quick results and large numbers, then getting involved in restoration work may be frustrating to you. Even those who value the vision of long-term work can be challenged by the lack of instant results over the course of supporting restoration projects.

On the flip side, let's say you have a desire for fewer, but deeper relationships, and you value the process and messiness of relational work. Simply saying hi to someone as you hand out food items through relief work may feel frustrating. Perhaps you have seen the impact of what creating a community around a homeless person can do for them, how it can open the door to their desire to grow.

＋ NPO ＋ = Impact

You desire to be part of something that will equip them and help them become independent in the years to come. A program that may take years to complete, but will result in their complete self-sufficiency and their investing back in others in that community. That is restorative.

Relief work is typically easier for someone to start volunteering with. A nonprofit can more easily create on-ramps for volunteers through relief work. A nonprofit who does work across all three R's might look for ways to begin with relief work volunteer opportunities. They can then use those to build relationships and educate volunteers about the value of their restoration work. They are helping volunteers move across the spectrum from relief to restoration.

However, when an organization that focuses on rehab or restoration work creates entry points in relief work but does not move volunteers or supporters toward rehab and restoration, they end up with supporters who do not value the primary services the organization provides. There becomes a disconnect in the partnership.

Let's say the inner-city kids mentoring program does a quarterly meal delivery outreach to neighborhood homes that attracts a large number of volunteers. If the nonprofit does not develop these meal delivery volunteers in education or awareness about the after-school mentoring, there will ultimately be a disconnect. These volunteers will only know the nonprofit for the meal delivery outreach and therefore view them as a relief organization. The volunteers do not have a vision for serving 30 children in a deeper and more comprehensive way because they are passionate about providing meals to hundreds of neighbors. They do not connect with the actual vision the organization was designed for, which is breaking a culture of poverty, and feeding is simply a gateway to that deeper picture of impact.

As donors, many of us, have been pre-programmed to think about giving from a relief standpoint. We typically think of success as larger numbers, less cost-per-person, etc. If we as donors unknowingly take a relief mindset into a restoration model, we create a system that is at odds with itself. If a donor serves as a board member but is not educated on what a restoration model looks like, then the board can make decisions based on a relief mindset, which contradicts with the very work they are trying to do. The organization is then operating without a full context of understanding. They are applying their comfort zone of relief to a restoration model.

An organization that understands its fit among the three R's can educate its donors about the work they do. They can bring on board members who connect and resonate with their model. They can create partnerships where everyone is moving in the same direction.

You as a donor can ask the organization questions about how they function in the three R's. While this may be a new concept to some nonprofits, others may even be able to say, "30% of our work is relief, 20% is rehab and 50% is restoration." You could consider it their "portfolio" of change.

Clearly understanding this would have a huge impact on your view and understanding of that organization. As a result, it would have a huge impact on knowing your potential fit with that organization.

Organizations in all three models of relief, rehab and restoration need partners, donors and advocates. That does not change. However, the intensity of the involvement and understanding that is needed increases as you move from relief to restoration.

The ideal partnership for an organization and donor is a long-term relationship around a common cause with a common vision of change. If the way they are both working to create change aligns, then the donor is ideally looking to stay long-term. They are not looking for an exit strategy, but are instead thinking, "Why would I want to go anywhere else?" The donor is not worried about the organization being "reliant" upon them, because they both want to foster a long-term relationship. They are thinking, "What kind of change could we make over 10, 20, or 30 years?"

CHAPTER 6

KNOW NONPROFIT ORGANIZATIONS

To find the right partners requires you to understand nonprofits, how they work and what types of organizations are the right fit for you.

Developing the right partners is key to finding your fit in philanthropy. To find the right partners requires you to understand nonprofits, how they work and what types of organizations are the right fit for you.

Nonprofits are the matchmakers between you and the cause(s) you care about. In this section, you will learn both what matters in nonprofit organizations and how nonprofits work.

What Matters In Nonprofit Organizations

Relationships

When it comes to philanthropy, everything boils down to relationships.

Relationships depend on trust.

And trust depends on correct understanding that comes through good communication.

John and Mary are a married couple in their mid-fifties. John noticed recently that Mary has become hard of hearing, so he called their family doctor and said, "Mary's losing her hearing, can you get her in to see an audiologist?"

The doctor replied back, "I can't get her in for six weeks."

John said, "She's going to be deaf in six weeks, we need to do something now!"

+ NPO + = *Impact*

So, to appease John, the doctor told him, "Well, you can range test her yourself to see how close you need to be before she hears you."

John decided to secretly test Mary that night in their house. Their open-house floor plan was the perfect space to experiment. John took a notebook out of his pocket, stepped back 30 feet behind Mary, and asked, "What are we having for dinner?" He waited. No response. He then stepped forward until he was 20 feet behind her and asked again, "What are we having for dinner?" John marked this in his notebook and moved 10 feet from her. "Mary, what are we having for dinner?" He waited, looking for some kind of body movement or turning. Nothing. So he moved just 4 feet from her. "Mary, what are we having for dinner?" He waited. After a couple seconds, Mary turned around and said, "John, for the fourth time, we're having chicken!"

Our understanding and assumptions play a key role in trusting anyone, and this is particularly true when it comes to nonprofit organizations.

As a donor, you need to be able to trust the organization. Trust is a key to all healthy relationships. Unfortunately, the nonprofit sector has a low trust factor. This is due more to perception than reality. When a breach of trust happens in one nonprofit, and is then shared in the media, that breach of trust unfortunately leads to mistrust of other organizations. They are guilty by association.

However, these issues are not the only reason trust is low regarding nonprofits. Another major issue harming trust is a very practical one—high turnover in leadership and development roles.

Leadership and development roles are the people with whom you build relationships at a nonprofit. Why is turnover so high? The average Executive Director has problems working with their board, so they stay an average of 4.2 years. The average Director of Development battles fatigue fighting short-term philosophies in their organization, so they stay an average of only 12-18 months! These factors lead to a lack of long-term relationships connected with the organization, which lead to a lack of trust in the organization.

For you to build trust with an organization, you need to build a relationship with them. You cannot depend on what has been said in the media, you must have correct understanding, just like John and Mary.

When problems (or even perceptions of problems) arise, if you have built a relationship, you can address these with someone you know and trust. Without a relationship, you will most likely just leave or make your own assumptions.

A story hit the media regarding questions about the amount of money being spent on staffing at a local organization. The assumptions played out in the media were the costs for the staff salaries were out of alignment with the number of children served. Jim, a donor who had given to the organization for the last 9 years, saw the report on the news. The next morning he picked up the phone to call Helen, the organization's Director of Development, and asked some questions about the news report. They discussed how the organization's counseling services were critical to the restorative work they did with the children. They were committed to long-term and relational services for each child to help them successfully graduate high school and college. This commitment brought a need for a wide variety (and depth) of services.

$$+ NPO + = Impact$$

Because of the phone call, Jim received clarity, increased commitment and was equipped with an ability to passionately explain the work of the organization to others. His strong relationship with the organization, through Helen, turned something that could have broken trust with him and others into a win for everyone.

However, when personal relationships with an organizations leadership, like Helen, are weakened due to high turnover, that organizations ability to weather the storms of mistrust and misinformation become more difficult.

Some organizations attempt to conceal their problems, flaws or even unethical practices, instead of addressing them within the context of relationship. However, the truth is they are already more transparent than they think they are, just not intentionally.

For example, our company only works with organizations that are referred to us. There are already relational connections there before we begin working with them. As we explore whether they would be good partners, I talk with members of the community connected to that organization's staff, board and supporters. Secrets that supposedly hide in the closets of these organizations are usually already standing out in the open.

The truth, whether as a donor or a nonprofit, can set you free to then build an authentic relationship, admit weaknesses and work together for the common good.

Relationships are not disposable. When a nonprofit treats its employees as disposable, the organization and the cause it serves both suffer. When we, as donors, treat our relationship with a nonprofit as disposable, the same is true. Relationship building is hard work, and for people to be served in the best way, relationships between the donor and the nonprofit partner are critical.

Relationships are designed to be long-term.

But here is the exciting part - you, as a donor, have the ability to create change within the organization you are partnering with. You can drive questions about valuing relationships and thinking about the organization in different ways.

Relationships create change. Bad relationships create negative change and dysfunction. Healthy relationships create positive change and impact.

Why Does This Matter To Me?

Understanding what a healthy nonprofit/donor relationship looks like helps you to:

1. *Know what a healthy organization looks like*
2. *Recognize red flags of unhealthy organizations*
3. *Understand what to expect and how to relate with a nonprofit*

Why Are Nonprofits Formed?

When a need or value surfaces in a society, business or government often work to address that need or value.

For example, let's say new home construction on the edge of town creates the need for closer groceries because the closest one is 10 miles away. Since the new housing is primarily made up of upper-middle-class residents, a chain grocery store will work to open a new location for them because the need (groceries) can be supplied by the business sector (chain grocery store) and paid for by the recipients (homeowners).

In that same example, the construction creates a need for city water and new roads to reach the new housing development. In this case, city government will provide this because the need (water and roads) can be supplied by the government sector (city government) and paid for by the taxes from this growing population (homeowners).

These are needs, but let's move this discussion to values. These same residents have expendable money and they value going out to dinner and watching movies. It is not a need, but it is something they value. As a result, new restaurants and a movie theater will open near them because the value (eating out and movies) can be supplied by the business sector (restaurants and movie theater) and paid for by the recipients (homeowners) who can afford it.

Now, let's turn this example around. Because many middle-class residents have been moving out to the edges of town for past 10 years, there are now fewer people living in the inner city. The majority of those who do are lower-income residents. The closest downtown grocery store could not afford to stay open and closed three years ago.

Due to a lack of public transportation and the fact many inner-city residents do not have reliable transportation, access to groceries and healthy produce is extremely limited. There is a need for closer groceries and healthy produce for those living in the inner city.

Unlike the new construction on the edge of town, it does not make business sense for a new grocery store to come in because history has shown these residents cannot support one. Therefore, this is not a problem the business sector can address. Because local governments do not typically play a direct role in grocery stores, it is not an issue the government sector can address.

Yet, access to groceries and produce for the inner city is a need in this community.

When meeting a need or value does not fit for the business sector or government sector, this is where the nonprofit/charitable sector becomes an important part to creating stable and vibrant communities.

In this community, a nonprofit food co-op organization could meet this need. It would require donations from those who believed in the cause to operate the co-op. Volunteers would be needed to operate the co-op at an affordable cost. It would require people sharing the need and the idea with their neighbors. This nonprofit food co-op would bring together people with a passion for providing access to healthy food. It would allow those living in the inner city access to healthier food and the many benefits the food would provide.

Unlike a grocery store, this food co-op's goal would not be to turn a profit (without donations, it would operate at a loss). Instead, the food co-op's goals are bound by their mission of providing affordable access to healthy groceries to those living in the inner city and by their vision of access to healthy food for everyone in their city.

A nonprofit is formed when a group of people believe a need exists and when there is a gap keeping this need from being met by business or government. A group of individuals then form a charitable nonprofit organization to fill this gap.

A for-profit business is driven by a financial bottom line. A business is designed to create a profit.

In contrast, a nonprofit is driven by a "mission and service bottom line." The services it provides do not create enough (if any) income to sustain itself financially. Without outside sources of funding, the nonprofit could not keep its doors open.

For example, the fees charged by the food co-op would not cover enough to sustain the organization. Therefore, it requires outside donations.

Since a nonprofit is designed to lose money in its mission-favored activities, the need for funding must be covered by other means. Depending on the type of organization, this includes things like earned income, fee-for-service, endowment revenue, grants, service fees, government funding and philanthropic fundraising.

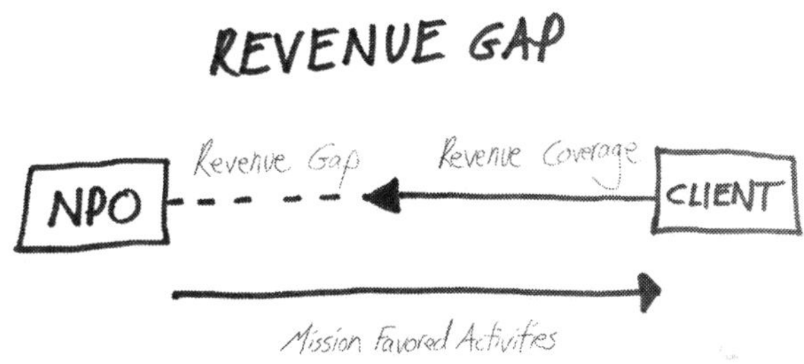

Revenue Gap:
Donors provide value through financial support, volunteering, leveraging networks, insight, advocacy and championing the cause. This can be covered through earned income, fee for service, government, endowment proceeds, fee for service or in-kind gifts.

Service Provision:
The organization provides value through social investment opportunities, recognition, opportunities for involvement and responsible stewardship of gifts.

$$\text{\includegraphics} + NPO + \text{\includegraphics} = Impact$$

The Three Pillars Of Philanthropy

Like we discussed earlier, philanthropy expresses itself in the three pillars of true philanthropy:

1. **Giving:** *The act of sharing your resources.*
2. **Volunteering:** *Freely giving your own time and giftedness/talents to a cause.*
3. **Advocacy:** *Championing something you value as much or more than yourself, connecting others to the cause and coming alongside those you care for.*

Volunteering, giving and advocating allow us to connect more deeply with what we care about. As we grow in these three pillars, we can more fully express and align our values with a cause we are passionate about and called to. Philanthropy can provide meaning and fulfillment in a way other things simply cannot.

Nonprofit organizations uniquely engage with all three pillars. Government and business cannot work with all three. As nonprofits provide the public good by engaging donors, volunteers and advocates in a cause they share, they ultimately create renewal in their relationships with donors.

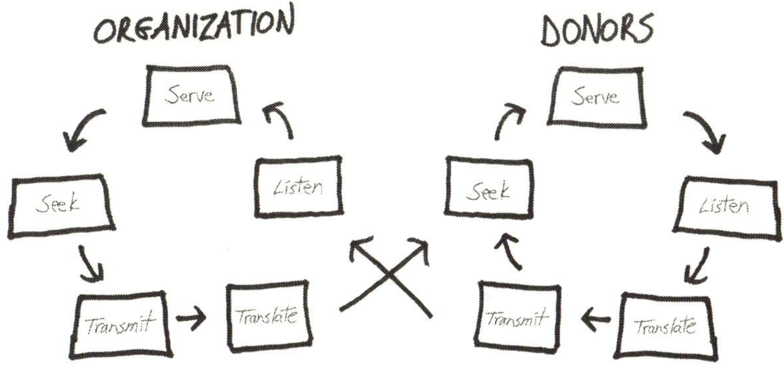

If we both love cats, then we share a common value and vision. You and I will both freely choose to invest ourselves in caring for cats. We do not need to be coerced. It will naturally spring from our hearts. As we invest together, we will discover a growing understanding and passion for cats. We will have a growing desire to care for cats and will be looking for an outlet to express that desire. We want someone to connect us to the cause.

Therefore, a nonprofit like the Cat Coalition can step in and meet that need for us. It is the vehicle for connecting people with common passions, like cats, and allowing those individuals the opportunity to express their passion by connecting their time (volunteering), resources (giving), and hearts (advocacy).

These three pillars work together to form a holistic expression of philanthropy. They do this through what we call transformational relationships—relationships that grow, "transform" both sides and renew themselves.

Elements Of A Healthy Organization

As an organization is created to connect people and resources to a cause, there are certain elements required for a healthy nonprofit. These elements span across the spectrum of donor trade-offs, 3R's, mission and vision.

These include, but are not limited to:

- *Board*
- *Staff*
- *Culture*
- *Fundraising*
- *Outcomes*

Board:

Because the board is designed to be the most passionate, intimate group of people in the organization, the health of the board is critical to the success of the mission. Signs of a healthy board include 100% of board members giving financially, members clearly understanding their responsibilities, members aligning and uniting toward the common vision instead of personal agendas and healthy communication between the board and Executive Director.

Staff:

The staff are the boots-on-the-ground team implementing the work. Signs of a healthy staff include a low turnover rate, staff members clearly understanding how their roles align with the vision, healthy communication among staff and healthy communication between staff and all other areas of the organization (board, donor, volunteers, and services).

Culture:

The culture of the organization is the true test of its health. A truly healthy culture should express itself in all areas of the organization (board, staff, donors, volunteers and services). Signs of a healthy culture include alignment behind the vision, open and honest communication and win-win relationships around the cause that are growing in depth, meaning and impact.

Fundraising:

Fundraising is obviously a foundational component of a nonprofit organization. Signs of healthy fundraising include alignment of funding behind the vision and impact pathway, donors progressing in their involvement in the three pillars and the growth of win-win relationships around the cause.

Outcomes:

Nonprofits are designed to create outcomes that impact a cause. Signs of healthy outcomes include: clearly articulating how the outcomes relate to both the need and the context of the need, evaluations regarding the specific outcomes, the capacity to change practices and strategies to improve outcomes as needed, and ultimately, increased ability to create impact.

How Nonprofits Work

Understanding the basics of how a house works can help you live in and maintain your home. In the same way, understanding the basics of how nonprofits work can help you develop stronger and healthier partnerships with organizations as you discover your fit.

Buckle up as we jump into the background and basics to gain a better understanding of how nonprofit organizations work.

Where Did The Formal Charitable Sector Come From?

Here is a quick history of the charitable sector:

- *The Revenue Act of 1894 established incentives to have defined, formal volunteer boards with tax-exempt status for nonprofits.*
- *The Revenue Act of 1954 established Section 501c(3) of the Internal Revenue Code (the designation for a tax-exempt charitable organization) and gave certain responsibilities to board members.*
- *The Not-for-Profit Organizing Act of 1971 defined the board as the core group of individuals responsible for the organization and provided formal guidelines for nonprofit boards.*

In 1904, there were only 138 registered nonprofit organizations![1]

Nonprofits now serve society in the form of charities, foundations, social welfare organizations, professional and trade organizations in 28 different classifications ranging from cemeteries to trusts to service providers.

While nonprofits can seem like a small subset of our economy, here are some interesting statistics:

- *Nonprofits account for 10% of all wages and salaries paid in the United States.* [2]
- *Nonprofit volunteers provide more than 8 billion hours of service time, creating more than $193 billion in economic value.* [3]
- *Foundations, through their grants, produce more than 500,000 jobs annually.* [4]

Who Leads Nonprofits?

Despite the varying types of nonprofit organizations, all share one thing in common. By law, every nonprofit is governed by a board of directors (or regents, trustees, governors, elders, etc.).

The board is the single most important group of any nonprofit. Not only are they legally responsible for the organization, they are also socially responsible for being good stewards of the organization's resources. They must make sure the organization's mission is fulfilled and that it operates as a trustworthy and effective steward of the resources entrusted to it by donors. Technically, the community "owns" the organization, and the board serves at the will of the donors. Board members are the most in-depth, legally charged advocates for the cause.

The highest purpose of a nonprofit organization is to act for the good of others—the community served by the organization. The nonprofit becomes the voice of those they serve. The board is charged with the responsibility to safeguard the public good. To accomplish this, a board must consist of committed individuals who fully understand their roles and obligations and who share a passion for the cause.

Nonprofit Costs: Direct Expenses + Indirect Expenses = Impact

Want to know how to create change through a nonprofit? The following equation is crucial for you as a donor to understand. A lack of this understanding results in frustration for both donors and nonprofits, ineffective partnerships, and ultimately, a lack of impact.

Understanding this equation, on the other hand, brings connection, trust and impact for a shared cause.

Nonprofit expense equation:

Direct Expenses + Indirect Expenses = Change

Now, let that sit a minute while we switch gears temporarily.

Let's say instead of a nonprofit, you are in charge of a cat food company, Cat's Cuisine. Your goal is to provide the most healthy and fresh cat food available on the market. You want to get this food into the mouths of millions of cats in the next five years.

What steps would you take to make sure this organization achieves its goal?

You might invest in:

- *Marketing*
- *Distribution*
- *A system to bring in and train the best employees possible*
- *Improved technology to improve quality and decrease costs*
- *A new manufacturing facility*

Whatever impact your organization is working toward (represented by the smiling faces), the chart and equation below illustrate how ALL expenses are needed for impact:

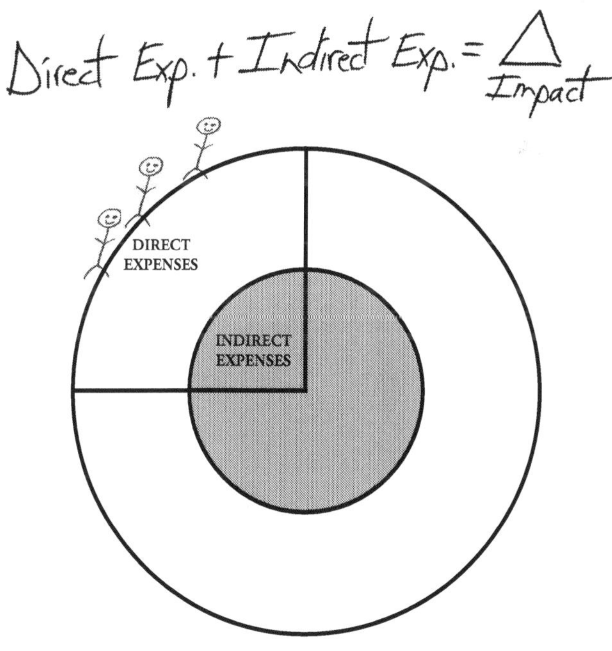

These things are called infrastructure. They are not the actual cat food itself, but they improve the organization so that it can better produce and sell the cat food. They would be considered indirect costs. On the opposite side, direct costs would include things like the food ingredients, cans and labor (actual cat food costs).

Investing in these indirect costs helps grow and improve your ability to accomplish the goal of getting this healthy food into the mouths of millions of cats in the next five years.

Let's now switch back to our nonprofit, the Cat Coalition.

Is infrastructure needed to accomplish your goal? Of course.

The Cat Coalition needs training materials, communication materials, accounting, transportation, phone systems and much more. These are all infrastructure needs to allow their direct services to happen. These indirect costs are part of the process.

Yet, many tend to applaud nonprofit organizations who minimize their infrastructure as more "mission-focused" or "efficient" with donations. Some nonprofits then say things like, "100% of your donation goes directly to services" instead of overhead.

Let's go back to the Cat Coalition. Which of their expenses actually help impact the cats? Answer: All of them!

To change lives, we must have both direct and indirect costs, not just one. The donor who restricts their giving to a direct expense can only receive the value of creating change if they are a subsidized by another donor who is willing to fund both indirect and direct expenses.

If every donor restricted their funds to direct services, then the organization would be unable to exist. They would have services, but no supplies, staff, facilities, systems, plans or utilities to run them.

Yet, many still champion the ideas that restricting donations and minimizing indirect expenses help increase impact on their donations.

Why is this?

This is most likely a reaction to abuses and irresponsible spending of some nonprofits that have been highlighted in the media. Therefore, operating on as lean a budget as possible can sound like a more worthwhile investment, because it appears the organization is a "better steward" of donations.

But if we think about our Cat Cuisine company, would "starving" the infrastructure help accomplish their goals? Of course not.

It would hinder them from getting their food to millions of cats:

- *Fewer people would be aware of, or have access to, this healthy food for their cats*
- *Poorly trained leadership would make poor decisions*
- *Employee turnover would increase*
- *Quality issues would increase*
- *Costs would increase*

In the same way, starving the infrastructure of a nonprofit hinders their ability to make an impact on the cause. Yet, the researchers at Nonprofit and Voluntary Sector Quarterly show us this is the unfortunate model we are finding in the nonprofit sector and it is causing very negative impacts as they try to grow.[5]

We see the results in many organizations like:

- *Poorly trained leadership making poor decisions*
- *Lack of clear communications*
- *High employee turnover*
- *Lack of process and systems development*
- *Decreased impact*

While I can certainly understand the attraction to "starving" infrastructure to build trust with donors, there is a much better way to gain trust.

Build Relationships

The core problem of the abuses and irresponsible spending of those organizations highlighted in the media is not they spent money on infrastructure. The core problem is a break of trust. Donors trusted these organizations to wisely steward their donations to make as much of an impact as possible toward the cause believed in. When those funds were recklessly or unethically used, trust was broken.

Therefore, the core issue for other nonprofits to gain trust is to build relationships. When donors have an authentic relationship with an organization and with the leadership of the organization, then trust is gained. Building that trust includes transparency regarding finances.

If a question arises, then a donor can simply talk with someone in the organization to find the information they need.

Restricted Donations – It's Still About Relationships

While nonprofits certainly have a responsibility for the negative impact of devaluing infrastructure, donors can mistakenly contribute to it as well.

When a donor or foundation restricts their funds to direct services, they can unknowingly rob the critical infrastructure needed to support the very services they want to support. They want the benefit of seeing impact with their direct service donation without investing in the whole process that makes the direct service possible.

For example, if a donor wants to sponsor an orphan overseas, but restricts their donation to cover food, clothing and education, they are therefore not supporting the whole process that makes providing food, clothing and education possible. The whole process includes staff to manage the projects, administration to coordinate logistics, financial accounting and auditing to keep finances legal and correct, travel to these countries, negotiating equipment prices, training volunteers, communications and much more.

The food, clothing and education cannot take place without the whole process functioning.

When a donor restricts their funds to direct services, they are actually being subsidized by other donors who are providing funding for the indirect costs. Other donors are investing in the infrastructure and overhead, which allows this donor the reward of seeing the full impact while giving a restricted gift.

I do not say this to make anyone feel guilty. I can also definitely respect taking precautions if someone has broken trust with you in the past. However, let's look at the big picture. The big picture is it takes the whole process to make an impact. Therefore, as donors, we need to invest in the entire process that leads to impact.

So, what is the magic number of how much budget goes toward impact?

100%.

If an organization is operating correctly, then ALL its resources are invested in the impact. All are helping to accomplish the mission and vision. Just like the Cat Cuisine's infrastructure, all indirect costs of a nonprofit (development, marketing, leadership training, utilities and administration) are being strategically invested for the highest level of impact.

If any cost does not contribute toward this goal, it should be cut.

Donor Bill Of Rights

In your partnership with an organization, there are certain expectations you should have of the nonprofit. We call these the Donor Bill of Rights.

1. *To be informed of the organization's mission, of the way the organization intends to use donated resources, and of its capacity to use donations effectively for their intended purposes.*

2. *To be informed of the identity of those serving on the organization's governing board, and to expect the board to exercise prudent judgment in its stewardship responsibilities.*

3. *To have access to the organization's most recent financial statements.*

4. *To be assured their gifts will be used for the purposes for which they were given.*

$$\text{You} + NPO + \$\$\$ = Impact$$

5. *To receive appropriate acknowledgement and recognition.*

6. *To be assured that information about their donations is handled with respect and with confidentiality to the extent provided by law.*

7. *To expect that all relationships with individuals representing organizations of interest to the donor will be professional in nature.*

8. *To be informed whether those seeking donations are volunteers or employees of the organization.*

9. *To have the opportunity for their names to be deleted from mailing lists that an organization may intend to share.*

10. *To feel free to ask questions when making a donation and to receive prompt, truthful, and forthright answers.*

Developed by: American Association of Fundraising Counsel (AAFRC), Association for Healthcare Philanthropy (AAHP), Council for Advancement and Support of Education (CASE), Association of Fundraising Professionals (AFP). Initial endorsers: Independent Sector, National Catholic Development Conference (NCDC), National Committee on Planned Giving (NCPG), National Council for Resource Development (NCRD), United Way of America.[6]

CHAPTER 7

KNOW HOW TO BUILD HEALTHY PARTNERSHIPS/ RELATIONSHIPS WITH NONPROFITS

*You are now
ready to begin
clarifying your
personal giving
philosophy and
defining what
a healthy
partnership
looks like
for you.*

Now that you have an understanding of both yourself and nonprofits, you are ready to begin clarifying your personal giving philosophy and defining what a healthy partnership looks like for you.

You are also ready to evaluate potential nonprofit partners on key areas of health and determine whether you could be a good fit.

My Giving Model

**KNOW YOURSELF
+ KNOW THE ORGANIZATION
+ KNOW WHAT PARTNERSHIP LOOKS LIKE
= MEANINGFUL IMPACT**

Fill in the charts on the following pages to clarify your unique giving model.

My 9 Donor Trade-Offs

Put an X where you believe you are on the continuum:

Efficiency _______________ vs. _______________ **Effectiveness**

Focus _______________ vs. _______________ **Flexibility**

Capacity _______________ vs. _______________ **Capability**

Speed _______________ vs. _______________ **Thoroughness**

Solutions _______________ vs. _______________ **Systems**

Unique _______________ vs. _______________ **Standard**

Independent _______________ vs. _______________ **Collaborative**

Experiment _______________ vs. _______________ **Investment**

Leader _______________ vs. _______________ **Organization**

MY FIT IN THE THREE R's			
GUIDE POINT	RELIEF	REHAB	RESTORATION
Collaboration			
Engagement			
Scale			
Numbers Served			
Relationship to Those Served			
Timeline of Change			
Impact			
Measures of Change			
Change Process			
Instant Gratification			
Difficulty to Raise $			
Equipping/ Education			
Skill			
Staff Concentration			
Efficiency			
Cost of Change (Admin Ratios)			

My Vision

My Passion

My Mission

____

____

____

My Values

____

____

____

My Interests

____

____

____

My Linkage/Connections

____

____

____

Additional Thoughts On My Giving Model

____

____

____

____

____

____

____

____

____

____

____

____

+ NPO + = Impact

My Giving Philosophy: Impact/Vision/Mission

My Questions For Nonprofits

- *How do you measure outcomes and successes?*
- *How does the board of directors function?*
- *Does 100% of the board give financially?*
- *What are your needs?*
- *What does growth look like for you?*
- *Where do you see your services fitting on the relief, rehab, restoration spectrum?*
- *What does efficiency and stewardship look like to you?*
- *Who do you collaborate with?*
- *What would happen to the organization if the CEO leaves tomorrow?*
- *How do you care for donors?*
- *Do you have succession plans in place for leadership and key staff?*
- *Are you spending enough on staff to create real change in your programs?*

Other Questions

____

____

____

____

____

Building My Giving Guide

This entire section has been the process of building your personal giving guide. Write down a simple paragraph that summarizes your giving model and philosophy. Then use this guide as you explore potential partnerships/relationships with nonprofit organizations.

____

____

____

____

____

____

____

____

____

____

____

+ NPO + = Impact

MY NONPROFIT ASSESSMENT TOOL	
AREA OF EVALUATION	**RATING 1-10** *(10= fully satisfied/ congruent, 1 = unsatisfied)*
AREA 1. MISSION, VISION AND CORE VALUES • They are both defined and clear and have clarity on when or how to say "no" to things • What does sustainability look like; what does success look like • How are they used (in org decision making) and how were they developed • Active strategic plan • Mission, vision/values are contextualized; they understand the problem they are addressing • How do the mission, vision and values align to my personal ones • Hedge Hog is clear (the three circles – excellence, passion and economics overlay)	
AREA 2. EQUATION OF CHANGE AND IMPACT • Defined what true change/even systemic change (success) looks like – changing the environment of the issue and how they measure it, testimonials to support it • Change is sustainable and their pathway of change is clear • Clarity of what collaboration looks like in creating impact • Outcome measures are clear and they understand how to handle failure	
AREA 3. BOARD CULTURE • Clear vertical alignment and engagement from board, to staff, to volunteers • Board is engaged, and functioning as a body of leadership, connected in value, passion to each other and know each other and adaptive in their leadership, 100% giving • Clarity on what the board relationship is like, term limits, terms, composition, etc. • How do they use and lead with the mission, vision and core values • Is a founder involved • Empowering the board to their potential as advocates building life relationships • Clarity on the boards role – as leaders and framers and reflects the community	
AREA 4. STAFF AND VOLUNTEER CULTURE • Knows what staff and volunteers like and sees them as assets • People, including volunteers, are aligned to the vision • See staff, board, and volunteers as life advocates in partnership w/mission/vision • Clarity of how to develop human capital and understanding of staff turnover • What is your ideal next hire and why • What does evaluation, transparency, and feedback look like with your staff	
AREA 5. PHILANTHROPIC SUSTAINABILITY • Defined CEO time allocation – focus on donor relationship growth • Defined what relationship retention and succession looks like – staff, donors, volunteers • Focus on creating life advocates for the cause as the end game • Operates from a place of sustainability, as opposed to crisis management • What is the role of the donor and what value does the donor create • What % of volunteers are donors and vice versa • A growing portion of the donor base has more than 5-year donor tenure • Clarity of the donor thank you/stewardship process and how to manage relationships	
AVERAGE SCORE (total divided by 5)	

NOW WHAT?

Healthy relationships around a shared cause can create transformation in the organization, the donor and those whom the organization works to serve.

Congratulations, you have now equipped yourself with valuable tools to take with you on your "giving for impact" journey. You have learned about yourself, nonprofit organizations and healthy partnerships. You have explored new perspectives, completed charts and reflected on your role in philanthropy.

So, now what?

First, I encourage you to look back through your answers to the questions throughout the book. Take time to process them and ask yourself, "What does this say to me?"

Some things may become immediately clear. Some may grow clearer over time.

Second, remember finding your role in loving people, philanthropy, is a lifelong pursuit. As you journey, you will discover passions, relationships, meaning and fulfillment you simply would not have found otherwise. So take your time and stay open hearted and minded.

Third, take action. Even if you have not yet found your ideal fit or the ideal nonprofit to partner with, taking one step in the right direction helps you discover your next step.

With these three things in mind, remember:

Philanthropy is all about relationships.

$$\text{+ NPO + } = \mathcal{I}mpact$$

Nonprofits and donors are partners who build a relationship over a common cause. Nonprofits cannot treat donors as a commodity without harming the relationship and hurting the cause they both have in common. In the same way, donors cannot use nonprofits as a commodity, because that will also harm the relationship and hurt the cause.

Relationships are not disposable.

Relationships are transformational.

Healthy relationships around a shared cause can create transformation in the organization, the donor and those whom the organization works to serve. Those whom you are seeking to serve need you and the nonprofits you partner with to have healthy relationships. The cause you have a desire to impact needs healthy partnerships in order to make a difference. You need a healthy nonprofit to partner with. The nonprofit needs you as a partner.

Your giving can make an impact and your relationship can do even more.

INDEX

Chapter 1: You Want To Make A Difference. Now What?

1. Gallup, Inc. "Most Americans Practice Charitable Giving, Volunteerism." *Gallup.com*, 13 Dec. 2013, news.gallup.com/poll/166250/americans-practice-charitable-giving-volunteerism.aspx.

2. Warner, Judith. "The Charitable-Giving Divide." *Www.nytimes.com*, The New York Times Magazine, 22 Aug. 2010, www.nytimes.com/2010/08/22/magazine/22FOB-wwln-t.html.

Chapter 5: Know Yourself

1. Berman, Melissa A. "10 Trade-Offs Donors Face That Make Philanthropy Tough but Rewarding." *Www.philanthropy.com*, The Chronicle Of Philanthropy, 08 December. 2014, https://www.philanthropy.com/article/10-Trade-Offs-Donors-Face-That/152111.

Chapter 6: Know Nonprofit Organizations

1. Trattner, Walter I. *From Poor Law to Welfare State*. 6th ed., Simon & Schuster, Incorporated, 2018, p. 92.

2. Brice McKeever and Marcus Gaddy. "The Nonprofit Workforce: By the Numbers." *Non Profit News | Nonprofit Quarterly*, 13 Jan. 2017, nonprofitquarterly.org/2016/10/24/nonprofit-workforce-numbers/.

3. "The Value of Volunteer Time." *Independent Sector*, independentsector.org/resource/the-value-of-volunteer-time/.

4. "Economic Impacts of 2010 Foundation Grantmaking on the U.S. Economy." *The Philanthropic Collaborative: Economic Impacts of 2010 Foundation Grantmaking on the U.S. Economy*, www.philanthropycollaborative.org/economicimpacts/.

5. Gregory, Ann Goggins and Howard, Don. "The Nonprofit Starvation Cycle." *Www.ssir.org*, Stanford Social Innovation Review, Fall. 2009, https://ssir.org/articles/entry/the_nonprofit_starvation_cycle.

6. "Donor Bill of Rights." American Association of Fundraising Counsel, 1993.

Jamie works as President and Director of Vision for JDLevy & Associates, a consulting firm dedicated to helping organizations devoted to doing good reach their true potential. Jamie, his wife, and three children live in Jasper, Indiana.

JDLevy & Associates' services focus on four key areas:
- *Vision*
- *Culture*
- *Impact*
- *Sustainability*

Learn more at jdlevyassociates.com.

Made in the USA
Las Vegas, NV
01 March 2023

68331327R00085